God's Glory and the Exhortation

AND

The Flames of God's Fire

Rene Bates

ISBN 978-1-64349-443-2 (paperback)
ISBN 978-1-64349-444-9 (digital)

Christian Faith Publishing, Inc.
832 Park Avenue
Meadville, PA 16335
www.christianfaithpublishing.com

There is a single bond that connects the prophets of God, and the link is, they always oppose the "traditions of men" in His church.

Printed in the United States of America

I was blessed as well as deeply impressed with the years of spiritual maturing and growth that it took to produce this kind of writing. A reader could not fail to be touched by the Lord in any number of ways in your collection of reflective essays.

—Charlie Johnson,
Manager of Christian Books Publishing House,
The Seed Sowers

Intriguing blend of spiritual vignette personal testimony. The author makes numerous thought-provoking statements. Author Bates has a timely, and probably convicting for many, message to share.

—George Allen,
Journalist for *The Christian Advocate*

I was touched in my spirit by what the Lord gave you to write. I'm sure all the messages that you gave from your heart originated from the heart of the Father. I want to confirm that I personally believe God's anointing was in this writing. Your humility and honesty were apparent.

—Betty Daffin,
Staff of *Last Days Ministry Magazine*

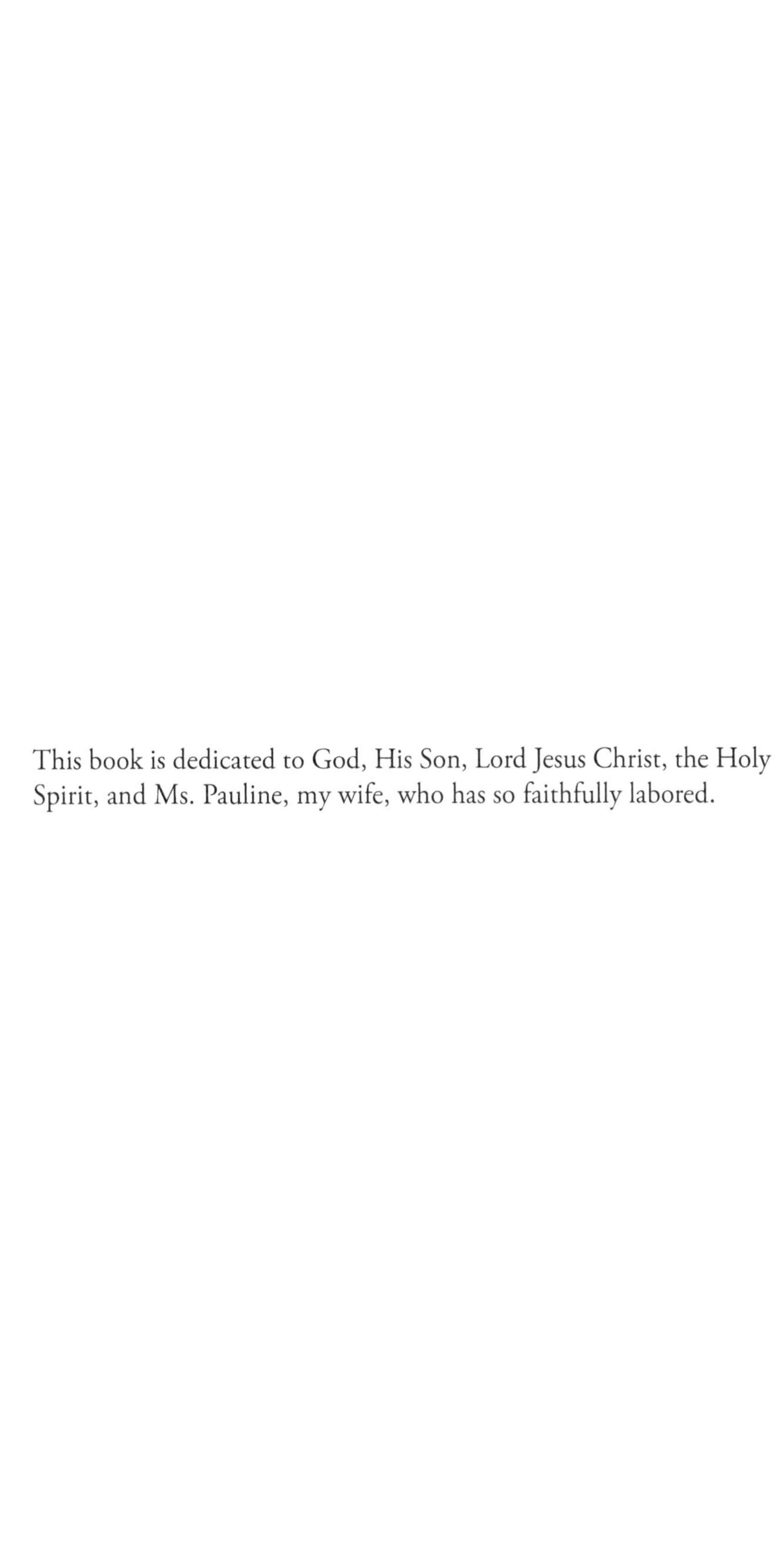

This book is dedicated to God, His Son, Lord Jesus Christ, the Holy Spirit, and Ms. Pauline, my wife, who has so faithfully labored.

The reason Jesus Christ and the Apostles were first persecuted and then killed. For this reason, the Jews persecuted Jesus and sought to kill Him, because He had done these things on the Sabbath.

—John 5:16 / Mark 7:6–9 / Colossians 2:8

Author's Note

> For God may speak in one way, or in another, yet man does not perceive it.
>
> —Job 33:14

> He who has an ear to hear, let him hear what the Spirit says to the churches.
>
> —Revelations 3:22

> You are our epistle written in our hearts, known and read by all men, clearly you are an epistle of Christ, ministered by us, written not with ink but by the Spirit of the living God, not on tablets of stone but on tablets of flesh, that is, of the heart.
>
> —2 Corinthians 3:2–3

Contents

God's Glory and the Exhortation

Contents
The Flames of God's Fire

Chapter One
Qualifications

It isn't profitable to speak about oneself, but here is a little about me. My name is Rene Bates. I'm fifty-two years old and have been married to my wife, Ms. Pauline, for thirty years.

On March 30, 1978, at 3:30 p.m., the hand of God touched my life. I felt as if I would explode as wave after wave of His Spirit was breathed into me. Six months later, I asked Him if I should go to Bible school.

"No," He replied, "I will use life to teach you."

As I look back on it, I see His divine wisdom and guidance for me. He was the one who saved me, and He is the one who trains me. I've been with Him all these years in the desert, waiting, listening, being broken and purged by His wonderful fire, which will transform me into His image.

I have no qualifications—I simply reflect His love, by which He first loved me. If I suffered, it was only because my Lord wanted to teach me obedience. Sometimes, I am slow to learn.

If there is anything good or noble in my life, it's Him, not me. He teaches me to be still, like a calm pond, so that when He speaks, ever so softly and sweetly, I respond as if a small pebble was dropped into the middle of a pond.

It is as if His hand pours me out before the four winds of heaven. His cross is the place of my habitation. I must always embrace the word and the death that truly brings life. His love is so pure and unselfish that, at times, I can only weep before Him. To know Him is to love Him.

He wounds only that he may eventually heal, and He grants many blessings through brokenness. If I should live out my days alone in the desert, then I should bow my knees to the Holy One and accept, from His precious hands, whatever He ordains for me. The sorrows of this life become the jewels in His crown, while the tears become the dew that waters heaven.

Rene means "reborn" or "born again."

For after these many years, the Lord spoke very quietly to my heart regarding the reason He chose me to write at this time. "I chose you because of the qualifications you do not have, that I may fill you with Mine." Knowing that, I bring before you the quill and the cross.

Chapter Two
Resting Deeply in Him

It seems to me that many people are shallow to the deeper things of God through no fault of their own. Did you ever meet anyone who quoted scripture verses, one after the other, but you sensed no depth to the conversation? The impression leaves one with the feeling of being three miles wide and only one inch deep. Serving God and the business of serving God will be revealed.

To understand the deeper side of God, one must not rely on his own knowledge. Through time, he must receive what God gives to those of humble standing. He does that to reveal His great graces. We often wish to perform a great feat. Should we then compete with our Lord, when only He is deserving of attention? We must lay aside all that seeks to draw notice to ourselves. It's not important for us to see everything He's doing in our lives; we must simply believe He is constantly bringing us closer to Him. It's better to be still, to quiet our thoughts and desires, and to know that He is God. The highest form of prayer is to stop asking Him to make us comfortable and rich, as if He exists for our pleasures, and to resign ourselves to whatever He desires for us. We should begin to praise Him in all things.

Do not be surprised when you sin. That is false humility and pride. You should know that everyone has faults. Only Jesus can deliver us from endless sins. If we fail, that should only humble us and drive us to the cross of mercies, knowing His love and blood will forgive us. The most blessed life is one lived in a state of grace, where nothing bothers you. No tribulation or sickness can overtake or dishearten you then. One learns to be quiet and stops striving to accomplish great deeds, knowing, in the end, little will become of those. Instead, one begins to know the truth, our Lord, and one begins to walk a life of holiness and freedom.

Our highest goal should be to die to ourselves for His sake. Love of ourselves destroys fellowship with Him. It's time to know Him, not simply know about Him.

God is in everything but sin. Whatever happens to you first goes through His hands. If you're afflicted, it's for His sake and your own good so that He may wash you through the waters of affliction. He's never closer to you than when you sense He has left. He wants you to search Him out, to draw close to Him, and finally, when He reveals Himself to you, the embrace is even more sweet. Don't worry what your flesh says—your spirit is one with His. All things will end soon, anyway.

Your greatest enemy is yourself, because the self is deceptive. We tend to think we're good, but only God is good. If there's anything good in us, it's Him, not us. What good is boasting? Don't answer an attack against yourself, lest your pride shows. If you realize you're nothing, nothing will bother you. Remain passive in Him and let Him live His life through you. Cease to live for Him. Search out wisdom, and she will be good to you.

Don't rely on yourself or even be conscious of yourself. Give yourself to His ever-outstretched, nail-pierced hands to draw you to His bosom. Don't just study the scriptures—give yourself to Him with unconditional love. He would ask, "Do you really love me?"

Scripture knowledge without love begets pride, the worst of all sins, because it's so deceptive. If you're prideful, you rarely know it. If you're humble, you'll probably be unaware of it. Give your heart to Him, that He may make it pure, then the words you speak will be spiritual, giving life to those who hear them. He who is joined to the Lord is one in spirit with Him.

Those who speak from themselves seek their own glory and give stones instead of bread, serpents instead of fish. Stones are heavy and give no nourishment. The serpents that come from people's mouths create lust even as they speak. Our hearts must be pure, then our words will be spirit and will give life, not poison.

Chapter Three
The Infinite God

As we begin to see God in everything, He reveals Himself in everything—except sin. We should see Him in His creation: the trees, the oceans, the gentle kiss of a summer breeze, or the powerful wind of a winter storm. Everything is a shadow of the Creator.

As He made seasons of summer, fall, winter, and spring, so are those reflection of a Christian life. Summer is the time when all seems bright and full of life, but soon, a Christian finds himself in the fall of his experience, when everything seems to be losing life. He might even sense the approach of death.

Suddenly, he's in winter. There are no leaves or fruits on the trees. Yet during winter, the tree renews itself inwardly, and there is still life. Springtime comes in all its glory, and the tree buds again. Summer arrives. The cycle is complete, but not ended, and so it is with a Christian.

A Christian is like a stream then a river. God is like the ocean, vast and deep. The river's ultimate goal is to empty itself into the ocean, and so we must lose ourselves in God, that He may be all and in all.

We're like the wind that doesn't control where it's been or where it's going. Only God's breath, breathed into us, directs our paths. We must give ourselves to prayer and ask that He gives us ears to hear and eyes to see Him in everything. Prayer is speaking, listening, and seeing. The early church prayed. The members never prepared anything because they never knew what would happen. Why do we know what will happen at meetings and when? That tells us who's in control. Everything is predictable.

So many sermons are prepared speeches from men's intellect. That's why people can't remember them. The speaker parrots a tape or book for his prepared speech. I learned that Jesus just sat down and talked, as did the Apostles. They spoke from within and gave the Holy Spirit freedom to speak.

Chapter Four
Two Kinds of Love

There are two kinds of love—conditional and unconditional. The first kind says, "I'll love you if you'll love me." It also sets time limits.

The second kind says, "I'll love you no matter what you do. You don't have to love me back. You're free."

God loves us, not because of who we are, but because of who He is. God is love.

Eventually, love must find its way back to God and love Him for who He is. Love never dies. It goes ahead and waits for us.

If you would fix your heart completely on the love of God, He would remove your carnal pleasures and grant festivals of jubilation and celebrations of divine light and joy.

The world has considered some to be worthless, while others are reckoned as fools for Christ. All of us must someday pass from the present to the eternal. One should let the essence of God's infinite bliss and the brilliance of His glory draw one to His heart. He's in eternity and wishes us to join him there with absolute devotion.

> Dear Jesus, I'm taken captive by Your heart, and I desire to repose there forever. May I absorb more of You that I may present You to others. Only Your love can satisfy the passionate yearning of my heart. I am Yours. Touch me with Your love. Amen.

Chapter Five
Two Kinds of Hearts

> There are two kinds of hearts—pure and clean.
> Blessed are the pure in heart [not the clean in heart].
> —Matthew 5:8

Pure is single, not mixed. Many have clean hearts. They love Jesus, but they also love what they get from Him. If a Christian was asked "Why do you love Jesus?" he would probably reply "Because He saved me."

That is a mixture. Instead, the response should be "I love Him for who He is, not because of what He gives me."

Wouldn't you want your children to love you that way? Even if He says "You must go to hell for eternity," our response should be "Because You are beautiful and holy, then yes, Master, if that is Your decision."

Blessed are the pure in heart. If we bear the stigmata of Christ within our hearts, we shall receive life from death, consolation from desolation, and spiritual sweetness from the celebration of life.

The active heart is busy about many things, but the contemplative heart rests at Jesus's feet, listening with a soft heart—in peace.

Chapter Six
Two Kinds of Prayers

There are two kinds of prayers—selfish and unselfish. Selfish praying says, "Give me this. Can I have that? Bless me. Take away all pain and discomfort. Come to Jesus and be happy always."

Unselfish prayer says, "I love you, Jesus. I place my life in your hands. Do with me as You will."

As the sun melts the snow, so do prayers inflame our hearts from the ice of imperfection and the coldness of sensual self-love. God doesn't ask for many words, only our hearts in prayer.

Chapter Seven
Two Kinds of Crosses

There are two kinds of crosses—His and ours. Jesus said that if we were to follow Him, we must take up our cross, not His. It hurts. It cuts into our flesh, which is our self. We must go the way of sorrows too.

Some go to the cross kicking and screaming, and some go quietly, but all believers will go, one way or another. One command rings down through the centuries—"You can't be My disciple unless you take up your cross and follow Me."

We love His cross because that is where He suffered and where our sins were forgiven. What about ours? Do we love the fellowship of His sufferings and being conformed to His death? (Phil. 3:10).

At the cross, Jesus drew all men to Himself. Many are called to the cross, but few are chosen to be crucified by His love. Embrace it, and it will transport you to heaven.

Chapter Eight
Some of My Encounters in the Spirit Realm

I would like to relate a few experiences I've had in my journey to the cross of Jesus Christ and give a few glimpses into the eternal realm of the supernatural. Although, as a born-again Christian, I've been factually crucified with Christ (Galatians 2:20) experientially, we have to constantly go to the cross of life for life. I have been sent not by men or through men but through Jesus Christ and God, our Father.

May His divine light illumine and expose the shadow of sin.

Chapter Nine
The Dream

Approximately sixteen years before my conversion, I encountered, for the first time, my Savior and Lord Jesus Christ through a dream. I have some reservations in calling it a dream. Afterward, as I pondered it in bed, I wondered if it was a dream or if I actually experienced it.

My wife, Pauline, was in the hospital for minor surgery, and I was home alone in Maine. As I left the kitchen and entered the living room, I noticed someone standing outside the front door to my right. I immediately had a strong sense of twilight or dusk, the gray period between day and not-yet night. From outside came the sounds of a mob cursing angrily.

I opened the door and walked into the hall to meet the man standing there. He was my height and had his face lowered and turned slightly to the left.

"Will you hide me?" he asked.

I knew the mob was after him and, if I hid him, they'd come after me too, if they found out. I decided to risk it. There was an attic off the hall to the left. I led him there. "Hide in there," I said. "You'll be safe."

I closed the door and went back into the house.

By that time, it was so dark I could almost feel it. I kept hearing the angry, cursing mob outside. When I looked again, I saw they carried torches. I hurried to close all the shades and blinds. They were just outside my window. I was frightened.

I thought of the man. There was something about his eyes that was different, but I couldn't recall what it was. He wore a robe and had shoulder-length hair and a beard.

There's something about his eyes, I thought. *What? This can't be happening. I'm not dreaming, am I?*

I went to the bedroom to see if I was in bed, but I wasn't there. I slapped my face and hands and felt the shock. It was real.

I decided to visit the attic and look at the man again. When I went in, I didn't see him right away. Then I looked up and saw him sitting higher up with his face lowered. That time, he smiled. Again, I was struck by his eyes.

I closed the door and went back into the house. By then, I felt it was the gray time of dawn between night and day. Quiet descended.

I looked out the glass front door and saw the man leaving. I ran to open it as he walked down the steps leading to my apartment.

"Where are you going?" I asked.

He turned and looked over his right shoulder but not directly at me. "It's safe for me to go now."

"What's your name?"

"Jesus Christ." He turned and walked off.

I felt a jolt and found myself lying in bed. I remained there for hours, wondering if it was a dream or reality.

Chapter Ten
The Death that Brought Life

Fifteen years passed. Next, I received a call from my brother, Joe, concerning our mother. She was gravely ill, and Joe told me I'd better go to Maine and see her soon.

Pauline and I flew from Nevada to Maine. Joe met us at the Portland airport and drove us to the small town of Lewiston.

Before we went in to see my mother, Joe said, "She's been really sick. Don't be surprised when you see her, okay?"

We walked in, and she didn't look that ill to me. In fact, she looked pretty good. She held up her arms and hugged and kissed me, then she looked right at me with her pale-blue eyes. "Rene, will I be all right?"

I knew she'd believe whatever I told her. "You'll be all right, Mom."

With that, she kissed Pauline and Joe.

The next day, she slipped into a coma. I asked if I could spend the night in the room with her, and Joe said yes. At the time, I felt she was just resting and would recover.

The following evening, her breathing changed. I knelt beside the bed, my head a few inches from her face. Pauline was on my left, and Joe was at Mom's feet. I was clinging to her emotionally, unwilling to let her go. Suddenly, I saw fluid pour from her mouth, and although it hurts to admit it, I said, "Okay, God, you win. Please take her."

I immediately saw, from the top left side of the room, the Spirit of God. There was a very loud sound of flapping wings. He was very powerful yet gentle. My mother's spirit left her body as she gave her last breath, then her spirit united with God's Spirit; he appeared as a very bright light. Slowly my mom's spirit left her body and went into the light. My mom looked to be around thirty. Slowly the light moved around the top of the room as we watched in amazement. Then the Spirit left. I did not mention what I saw.

No one spoke for a few moments. We felt incredible joy and peace, whereas only moments before, we felt terrible sadness.

After a while, I asked, "Did you see what I saw?"

"I saw her spirit leave her body," Pauline replied.

"Yes," Joe said. "It united with God's Spirit and left."

We all saw it, not just me.

Our morning turned to incredible joy as we hugged one another.

There are those who will deny such a story and say "They just imagined it," but I can't deny what God did. Those two experiences happened before I was saved.

A very bright light.

Chapter Eleven
The Conversion

During the next year, I began reading the Bible for the first time in my life. I read the shortest books, one chapter at a time. I also began listening to a local Christian radio station.

One night, I heard a live talk program where people called in with Bible questions. Someone called and asked about the denomination I too was born into, and the host's answer offended me.

I'll call him and tell him off, I thought. *They won't know who I am. I won't give my name.*

I called, but the host answered so graciously that my anger melted. He finished with "Why don't you call me at eleven five, when the show's off the air? I want to talk to you."

"Fine."

I called back, and we talked. He invited me to his Bible study group on Tuesday nights, and I agreed to go.

On the next Tuesday, Pauline and I went to the house. We had a long discussion before going inside. I didn't want to go. She'd been saved since the age of nine, yet she loved me, who wasn't saved, anyway.

"Didn't you give your word you'd come?" she asked.

"Yes."

"Then you must be a man of your word."

I had the feeling that if I went in there, they'd try to make me like them or change me. I belonged to a different denomination and always thought I would.

We went inside. People smiled and said they were glad to see me. When they worshipped God in song, I suddenly realized they had something I didn't have. I wasn't convinced by their preaching; it was their form of worship that touched me. Years later, I learned that the pastor warned everyone not to say a word to me, because I would certainly resist any attempt at persuasion. God had told him I'd be saved, but I couldn't be pushed into it.

I attended the class for a few weeks, then on March 30, 1978, Pauline and I were eating at a restaurant. I couldn't seem to eat anything.

"What's wrong?" she asked.

"Is this stuff about Christ real? I have to find out."

We left the restaurant, and I drove without knowing where I was going. Suddenly, I saw a sign that read Christian Center. The building had once been a movie theater.

It was the middle of the afternoon when I walked in. A woman, whom I later came to know and love, said, "My name's Janice. Can I help you?"

"I want to know God," I blurted.

"The pastors have all gone home for the day. Just sit before the sanctuary and pray. I'll send someone to you."

I walked into the dimly lit room and knelt before the stage. Pauline knelt on my right.

I thought of the Lord and prayed, *Lord, where are you? Help me, please.*

I felt a sudden stillness. A hand touched my left shoulder, then another hand touched my right shoulder, then a third hand touched my head. People were praying softly.

Something very strong came into me and raised my feet even though my knees were still on the ground. I felt another wave pass through me, and I felt ready to explode. Something was trying to come out of my mouth.

Whatever it was, I knew it was good and came from God. Between waves of power, I felt glad for the chance to rest. I wondered if I might die.

A few moments later, another breath filled me, and that time, I overflowed. The words that came from me didn't come from my mind. My stomach was sore from the effort, and I never heard anyone speak in tongues before (1 Corinthians 12:10).

All I could do was keep repeating, "Thank You, Lord. Thank You."

When it ended, I felt weak from the experience, but I also felt clean. I was saved—my sins were gone. Janice told me later she saw fire around us, but my eyes were closed, and I didn't see it.

"Who prayed for me?" I asked.

She named two young men and herself, but I saw three young men leave with her.

Chapter Twelve
The Crucifixion

A few weeks passed, and I was again at the Tuesday night Bible study class. During worship, I sensed God saying He wanted to demonstrate His power and show those who where there something.

As the group of forty sang, the Lord gently lifted my head upward and stretched out my hands in the position of crucifixion. I knew God's power had come to me. I felt the crucifixion without the pain.

The Lord told me to reach for my Bible, which was on the floor beside me. I felt a power in my hands that I never experienced before or since.

With my eyes closed and head raised, my hands almost moved by themselves with surety and power. It was as though they knew what to do. As a new Christian, I had no knowledge of the Scriptures. I bought a copy of the Jerusalem Bible because it was written in modern English and made for easy reading.

As I was sitting there, I reached for my Bible, which was in a zippered vinyl case. I unzipped it, and the Bible fell open in my hands to reveal the pages God wanted. He told me the entire Bible was true but that those two pages were the heart of the Bible, the most powerful pages in the book.

I told the others, but I still didn't know what was on those pages. I knew God wanted them read out loud.

The others stopped singing.

"Please," I said, "I don't know which pages these are, but God wants them read. These two pages are the heart of the Bible, the most powerful in the book."

No one moved. I heard silence in the room as I sat there with my eyes closed and head up, my hands resting on the pages.

"All right," the pastor said. "Someone read it."

A man did. "They brought Jesus to the place called Golgotha, which means the place of the skull."

It was the crucifixion of Jesus Christ, His being mocked, His death, His burial, His resurrection, His great commission to us, and His ascension to the right hand of God (Mark 15:22).

After the first paragraph, the pastor asked the man to stop. I sensed he was frightened and wanted to regain control of the situation. I felt grieved. They wanted to know about Him, but they didn't want to know Him in a real way.

As I must give a full account to God, I tell you, I did not know what was on those two pages.

> And He did not do many mighty works there because of their unbelief. (Matthew 13:58)

Chapter Thirteen
The Fellowship of His Sufferings

Months passed. One Sunday, I was at a service, and as the pastor spoke, I felt ill. After the service, I went home and to bed. Within hours, I was seized by excruciating pain. It started in the upper part of the middle of my back and spread through me in waves. I never felt such pain before or since. It was so strong I couldn't breathe at times, and nothing helped.

The first night, Satan came to me. "Curse God, and I'll remove your pain."

"No," I replied. "The Lord rebuke you, Satan. The Lord Jesus Christ rebuke you!"

He left. Shortly thereafter, God spoke to me, "I'm letting you feel a little of what my Son suffered for you. I will take it away soon. This isn't a physical ailment, it's a spiritual one. Only I can deliver you."

I remained that way for three and a half days. Pauline invited two of her friends over to pray for me. By then, I felt as if the right side of my chest was crushed, while the left side felt filled with water. My face became bloated to almost twice its normal size.

Somehow, I got out of bed and sat in a kitchen chair. All three stood around me singing praise songs to the Lord and worshipping Him.

Suddenly, I felt warmth, as if a warm hand went up and down my back. The excruciating pain was gone. My chest and face shrank as quickly as a pricked balloon. I felt wonderful.

The Lord is good in whatever He does.

Chapter Fourteen
The Exorcism

Some friends once invited me to a charismatic fellowship at a Catholic church. I went expecting a chance to see what they did and to enjoy myself.

After the meeting, I was about to leave, and my friend came to me and asked if I'd pray for a woman.

"Where is she?" I asked.

He pointed. She sat on the other side of the building, with many pews between us. Ten people stood around her, laying on their hands and praying, but she was staring directly at me, not them.

I sensed a confrontation.

"Tell the people to remove their hands," the Lord said.

"Remove your hands from her," I said.

The people did, and two Catholic priests near the altar stopped and stared. Everyone knew something was about to happen.

"Greater is He who is within you than he who is in the world," the Lord told me. "Victory already is yours. It's just a matter of doing My work, but the power is Mine. Tell them."

I did, then I faced the woman. "The Lord rebuke you, Satan. Come out of her."

She laughed. "What do you think you're doing?"

"Say it again," the Lord told me. "This time, raise your right hand and point at her."

I did and felt power shoot from my arm into the woman. She gave a deep, long groan, and a four-foot pillar of smoke came from the top of her head and flew out of the building.

"If Satan came in by my eyes," she said, "he left by my eyes."

Although everyone else was filled with joy, the two priests left quickly. I never heard from them again.

Chapter Fifteen
The Miracle of the Arm

I recently attended a Bible study class sponsored by a church that had the reputation of being alive. I went to that fellowship before, but I learned they only wanted to control and magnify their so-called pastor. Their home study course, I heard, was more open.

As I sat in the person's home, the group began to worship, and I cried as I sensed the Lord move on me. He wanted to do something, but I didn't know what.

Suddenly, I had a vision of a hand and arm in a cast. "I will heal that man," God told me. "He's been unable to receive healing from men. Speak it, and I will do it."

I hesitated. I knew the pastors were waiting for something to accuse me of. No one in their group did such things, and there was no one there with a broken arm.

I took a step of faith and made the announcement. Although it seemed impossible, I knew it was God's voice speaking through me.

Twenty minutes later, two men and a woman came in. The second man had his arm in a cast. The power of God was present, and everyone felt it.

"Rene," someone said, "why don't you pray for him?"

Before doing so, I asked the man, "What's wrong with your arm?"

"I've been to three doctors, and the bones won't mend," he replied.

I put my hands on him and prayed.

After I finished, the man said, "I have a doctor's appointment this Thursday. I've had this cast on for three months."

During fellowship time afterward, the youth pastor came to question me. He and the other pastor didn't seem to believe what just happened.

"Why don't you come to church on Sunday like you used to?" he asked.

"I'm grieved when I see the Holy Spirit being quenched there."

He became offended. "God told us, the pastors and elders, that He would do no miracles at the church. He would only do them on Thursday night at home fellowships. Sundays are for teaching."

Have we fallen so low that we tell God what He can do and when? I wondered.

I left the meeting and never went back. The man with the broken arm received, from the Lord, a complete healing. When he saw the doctor on his next visit, he was completely healed and had the cast removed. The doctor said it was a miracle.

God is Spirit, and He's looking for some to worship Him in Spirit, not soul. I believe we have taken signs and wonders out of being Christian, substituting the spirit of intellect. If we have the written word, we can pick and choose, but God's spoken word is something men can't control, so they quench it.

If there are no signs and wonders confirming the spoken word on a regular basis in your fellowship, ask why not. I don't mean simple emotionalism or Christian fads like leg lengthening or blowing on people to make them fall down—I mean genuine signs, wonders, and miracles.

But never look to miracles; look only to Jesus. Don't even look to the one He uses; look only to Him.

Chapter Sixteen
Today

Pauline and I went to Yosemite National Park for a week of rest and meditation. Early one morning, we left our cabin and walked toward the cafeteria for breakfast when I saw, on my right, people laughing at a man who looked unusual. He wore a long green robe, was barefoot, and had long brown hair and a beard. He carried a staff.

The people who laughed were Orientals. They took the man's picture as they watched.

Pauline and I went into the cafeteria, got metal plates, and stood in line to be served. I was uncomfortable thinking of that pathetic young man. He was thin, while I was ready to eat as much as I wanted. Finally, so that I could eat in peace, I asked Pauline, "Would you take this money and give it to that young man outside?"

She turned and looked at me. "No. You do it."

I didn't want to get involved.

We got our breakfast, found a table, and prayed to give thanks for our food. I still felt uneasy and couldn't eat.

"Won't you take him some money?" I asked Pauline.

"God's dealing with you," she said firmly. "You get up and go to him."

I left in a hurry. By then, the tourists were gone, and the young man sat on wooden steps before the check-in area for cabins. He spoke to another young man on his right, and I didn't want to interrupt.

I walked around the yard, up the wooden steps and slowly moved closer, pretending to be reading the newspapers in their kiosks. When I was close enough, I heard the young man say, "God."

I moved closer and realized he was telling the other young man about God. I became angry. *He's in a cult!* I thought. *Just look at him! He's not like me. I'll test him.*

I moved until I stood over him. I felt incensed. "I heard you talking about God this and God that, but is Jesus Christ the Son of God?"

He shaded his eyes to look up at me and smiled. "Yes," he said softly. "He is."

When he spoke, I felt power leave the young man and come to me. I was surprised. His love was greater and stronger than my outward judgment of him. His skin and hair were weatherworn, but he had the whitest, straightest teeth I ever saw.

I regained my composure and attacked again. "All cults say Jesus is the Son of God, but I ask you, is He God, the Son?"

He smiled. "Yes, He is. Who is He to you?"

His love disarmed me again. It was much stronger than any man's hate. I sat beside him and told him who Jesus was to me. The young man on his right left, and the man spoke to me.

I never heard anyone speak the way he did. I met some famous Christians, but they were like me. He wasn't—he was very different. He quoted Scripture accurately and expounded on each one like no one ever did before. I tried to catch him in an error and failed.

His power of love was stronger, and I knew it. I submitted to him. He was more in the kingdom of God than me. We sat and talked for hours.

Pauline looked out the window at us occasionally, but she didn't interrupt. When I thought of a question, the young man answered before I could voice it.

I should go to my cabin and get my tape recorder so I can tape him, I thought.

"Never mind trying to tape me," he said immediately. "Your spirit's open to me and receives what I'm telling you. Don't worry about trying to remember what I say. Just remember that your words have power. They have strength. Be very careful what you say. You can never take them back."

By then, we moved from the steps to some large tree stumps. I noticed two attractive young women coming toward us. *If he looks at them, I'll know what's in his heart by his eyes*, I thought.

I leaned back and waited. They passed before us, and he saw them, but he didn't look at them. I was astonished. He wasn't showing love; he was love. That was his strength.

"Would you like to join my wife and me for breakfast?" I asked.

"You aren't ashamed of my appearance?"

"No." I hugged him and felt how thin he was.

We approached the table where Pauline sat. "Sit," I told the young man. "I'll get you something."

He ate thankfully.

Finally, I had the courage to ask, "What's your name?"

He looked into my eyes. "My name is Today."

That's odd, I thought. *Why not yesterday or tomorrow?*

"You are almost ready to receive the gift of exhortation," he said. "Pray that you receive it in fullness."

Finally, it was time to leave. Pauline and I were ready to travel back to Nevada. I didn't want to part company with Today.

He knew it. I offered him money, but he wouldn't take it. I hugged him and cried. I never experienced such love before.

"You have to go," he said. "You can go places I can't go, because of how I look."

That hurt. That was the lesson God wanted me to learn—never judge anyone by how he looks; the important thing is what he is.

When I was home, I found the following scripture:

> You are my son. Today [Jesus] I have begotten You. (Hebrews 5:5)

Multiple times Today is mentioned in the first five chapters.

Chapter Seventeen
God's Power

Two years ago, Pauline and I went to Grand Teton National Park. For six months, I had the feeling God wanted to show me something, but I didn't know what.

We went to the Grand Teton foothills before Jenny Lake. I sensed God's presence, and He called me in the Spirit, showing me a special place in the mountains. I had a vision of the valley and knew the path there, but He didn't ask me to come, because He knew I was so frightened I would disobey.

Instead, He said, "Once you start, you must not turn back There will be many obstacles, and you'll be afraid, but you must not turn back. If you do, you'll die. You can only preserve your life by coming to Me."

I decided not to go that time. Pauline stood beside me, and I knew God wanted me to go alone.

"I want to show you a little of my power," He said.

It was a crisp, clear spring day. Suddenly, up high, where God wanted me to go, a small dark cloud appeared. Within minutes, thick black clouds were everywhere, and lightning flashed. We felt His awesome power.

Suddenly, lightning struck to the right and the left.

"Please, God!" Pauline said. "I'm frightened!"

Hail the size of marbles fell.

"Lord," I said. "Please, no more."

It stopped as quickly as it began. I had my camera and photographed the mountain, but none of the pictures came out. All I had was pictures of hail. The next day, we were at the visitors' center at

Colter Bay. There was a Native American park ranger behind the huge desk, and under the glass was a picture of the entire Grand Teton range. He told me that the Native Americans in that area always knew there was one God and He had a Son, but they never knew the Son's name.

For hundreds of years, a young brave left the camp and went to a certain spot to meet God, searching for a vision from Him. It would always be for the good of others.

"Do you know where that spot is?" I asked. *It can be the same place God told me to go*, I thought.

"Yes." He pointed to the same place.

Pauline and I went back to Nevada at the end of our trip. For one year, I knew I had to go back and visit that spot. Finally, it was time. I was prepared to go that time.

Pauline walked me to Jenny Lake on a beautiful day. I was ready to say goodbye to her and leave.

Suddenly, everything was still. The wind died, and the lake was as smooth as glass. I felt God around me.

Last year, he said, "All I wanted was obedience. I watched to see if you made your first step, then I would've stopped you. You had to wait one year for this lesson. The place I want to meet with you is in your heart. That's the secret place, my son."

One day, I left home to look for my enemies and found no friends. I returned home.

Another day, I left home to look for my friends and found no enemies.

As a man thinks, so shall he be. Man feels most empty when he has completed his biggest fantasy and realizes that it didn't satisfy him. All is vanity. Fear God. Keep His commandments—that leads to life.

The one to come who causes trouble will be known as *omni*, every power.

Again, the word of the Lord came to me, saying,

> Son of man, speak to the children of your people and say to them when I bring the sword upon the

land, and the people of the land take a man from their territory and make him their watchman, when he sees the sword coming upon the land, if he blows the trumpet and warns the people, then whoever hears the sound of the trumpet and does not take warning, if the sword comes and takes him away, his blood shall be on his own head. He heard the trumpet but did not take warning. His blood shall be upon himself, but he who takes warning will save his life.

But if the watchman sees the sword coming but does not blow the trumpet, and the people are not warned, and the sword comes and takes any person from among them, he is taken away in his iniquity, but his blood I will require at the watchman's hand.

So, you son of man, I have made you a watchman for the house of Israel, therefore, you shall hear the word from My mouth and warn them for Me. When I say to the wicked, "Oh, wicked man, you shall surely die," and you do not speak to warn the wicked for his way, that wicked man shall die in his iniquity. But his blood I shall require at your hand.

Nevertheless, if you warn the wicked to turn from his way, and he does not turn from his way, he shall die in his iniquity, but you have delivered your soul. Therefore, you, of son of man, say to the house of Israel, "If our transgressions and sins lie upon us, and we pine away in them, how can we then live?"

Say to them, "As I live," says the Lord God. I have no pleasure in the death of the wicked, but that the wicked turn from his wicked way and live. Turn from your evil ways, for why should you die, oh house of Israel? (Ezekiel 33:1–11)

Chapter Eighteen
There Is a Difference

For the most part, we've had an irrelevant church in a decaying society that has stopped being salt to the world and, instead, joined it. There must be a change within the organized religions to a true devotion of faith in Jesus Christ as Lord.

Anyone willing to meet Jesus must be willing to go outside the camp, bearing His reproach (Hebrews 13:13). Many worship and are devoted to a set of religious principles and practices that have been placed on our shoulders as a heavy yoke. Through the traditions of men, we worship inanimate objects of our own reasoning instead of being devoted to the living Christ. We make a little god of what we do for Him as we worship our service to Him through our knowledge, piety, and structures of wood, hay, and straw. We're instructed to study and search the Scriptures, thinking that brings eternal life, but the Scriptures are to lead us to Christ. He alone is our Savior (John 5:39–44).

There's a difference between being devoted to our time with Him and simply being devoted to Him. There's a difference between reading His Word and hearing it. There's a difference between time spent for Him and time spent with Him. There's a difference between what men say He says and what He says. There's a difference between faith in God and common sense. There's a difference between simply wanting help from the world's pressures and wanting godly holiness. There's a difference between the sorrow the world produces and a godly sorrow producing repentance, which leads to salvation.

There's a difference between servants of the Lord and servants of the evil one. There's a difference between religious rites from men and a relationship with Jesus. There's a difference between gifts of the Holy Spirit and the offices in the church, and men's pride and all its deceptions. There's a difference between you choosing Jesus and Jesus choosing you (John 15:16).

There's a difference between the life, heart, and blood of Jesus and those of the justifiable self-respect of man. There's a difference between a clergyman serving a local church for pay and one who speaks by divine inspiration and utters godly rebuke on behalf of the One who sent him. There's a difference between a hired person whose motives are mainly mercenary and a servant of God who does menial jobs for the Lord's glory. There's a difference between hyping the crowd with loud shouting and true revival bringing repentance.

There's a difference between walking with the Lord and the strutting walk of a haughty, pompous hireling. There's a difference between praying to the Lord for His guidance on a matter, even if it goes against our interest or doctrine, and praying to the Lord to fulfill our own desires and beliefs, hearing only what we want to hear.

There's a difference between faith in one's faith and faith in God. There's a difference between the pastor of a flock and a prophet of God. There's a difference between this world and the next, just as there is between heaven and hell. There's a difference between the eternal counsel of God and that of man. There's a difference between the Old Testament and the New. There's a difference between the Jezebel paganism in the church and the sanctified people of God.

There's a difference between being of the world and simply being in the world, just as there is between living for Christ and living through Him. There is a difference between voting for your pocketbook and voting with the Book of Life, the Word of God. There's a difference between the worship before the throne of God and the worship before the altar of lust. There's a difference between the lost and the saved, the wicked and the just. There's a difference between the one who speaks God's word, wisdom, and righteousness and the one who speaks lying, deceitful, untamable mutterings.

There's a difference between the traditions of men that produce hypocrisy (Mark 7:6–9) and those handed down by the Apostles (2

Thessalonians 3:6–7). There's a difference between the unconditional love of God and the conditional love of men.

There's a difference between the greedy and the generous, the one who gives very little from the one who gives all he has. There's a difference between the one who uses Jesus, who, by stealth, will take His glory, and the one who gives Him glory. There's a difference between the one who serves God and the one who serves his own ministry, the one who desires leadership and the one who wants only to follow his Lord.

There's a difference between being anointed of God and being appointed by men, just as there is one between the fellowship of righteousness and the fellowship of lawlessness.

There's a difference between the coiled, twisted leviathan of fear and the peaceful rest in the lamb who takes away the sins of the world. There's also a difference between the righteousness one receives from religious laws and the righteousness that is through faith in Christ. There's a difference between the tree of life and the tree of the knowledge of good and evil, as there is a difference between the life of Christ and the death the crafty serpent brings.

There's a difference between judging a person by the outward appearance and hearing his words inwardly—out of the heart, the mouth will speak. There's a difference between salvation and damnation, as there is a difference between the old man and the new. There's a difference between Christians who are the one body of Christ and the clergy-laity doctrine of division. There's a difference between the whole body of Christ opened to be used in church and the closed meeting where only a few are in preeminence every week. Even though young people may teach in the church, there's a difference between them and their elders.

There's a difference between having an office in the church (Ephesians 4:11–12) and being called by that office (Matthew 23:7–12). There's a difference between one who's called by God to minister and one who transforms himself into a minister of righteousness (2 Corinthians 11:13–15). There's a difference between seeking the crowd and looking for the remnant. There's a difference between coming to Jesus for what can be gotten from Him, as the multitudes often do, and seeking Him for who He is.

Jesus answered them and said, "Most assuredly, I say to you, you seek Me, not because you saw the signs, but because you ate of the loaves and were filled" (John 6:26).

Christians, being the church, don't go to church; they are the church. There's a difference between what a person says and what he is, just as there's a difference between wanting to be a star and submitting to the Bright Morning Star. There's a difference between seeking the limelight and being in the light, as there is a difference between our way and the Lord's way. There's a difference between preaching and performing.

What can there be with no difference? There's no difference in how much the Father, Son, and Holy Spirit love you and are gentle with you. There's no difference in Jesus Christ—He is the same yesterday, today, and forever. He's our King, and His Word stands forever. He's forever unchangeable and is all-powerful and all-knowing. He is love, mercy, and truth, and He desires to enter your heart to become your personal defender and Savior. His goodness, love, and power await you.

Now there are diversities of gifts, but the same Spirit. There are differences of ministries, but the same Lord. There are diversities of activities, but it is the same God who works all in all (1 Corinthians 12:4–6).

Chapter Nineteen
Mike

Seven years ago, I had a personal experience that illustrates what happens when people stop serving God and start serving themselves—the plight of today's church.

One Sunday night, I went to a worship service at a church that I heard was right on target. Halfway through the service, I noticed a ragged, rough-looking man sitting to my right and a few rows back. He was a street person, with his right arm in a sling. He looked pretty bad off.

The pastor that night spoke about God's love to the packed house. I decided to talk to him after the service. With the customary up-tempo final song, the meeting ended.

As I moved toward the pastor, I heard God say, "I want to show you something. Watch."

People hugged one another, but when they saw the ragged man, they turned to others more like themselves—prim, proper, and clean. The elders and pastors did the same.

When the man walked toward them, they looked past him, even though he tried hard to get someone to speak with him. That continued for twenty minutes. He never knew I watched him, and I saw the rejection on his face.

Suddenly, he turned and walked out. I caught up to him in the parking lot.

"Friend," I said, "I saw you at the service and would like to talk for a few minutes, if I may?"

"I haven't eaten anything in three days," he replied. "My stomach hurts. I know those people think if they give me money, I'll buy drugs or alcohol with it, but that's not true. I was at the morning service and spoke with the pastor and a few elders afterward. I told them I hadn't eaten in three days. I asked them to send someone with me to McDonald's and watch me eat.

"They said, 'We give to the rescue mission.' I told them I had no way to get there. I'm too sick and weak. They gave me nothing."

The parts of his hand and arm in the sling were blue.

"What happened to you?"

"My clothes are dark and dirty. A few weeks ago, I was walking at night, and a car hit me. It wasn't the driver's fault—I walked right in front of him. Since then, I've been sleeping in the desert across this church. I was on my way to Phoenix, Arizona, because there's a second-start house there for Vietnam veterans. It's my last chance. No one will even buy me a hamburger. I can hardly walk."

"What did you do in Vietnam?"

"I was a gunner on a helicopter. I remember shooting women and children. I can't forget them. I started drinking after I got back to the States. My wife was a good woman, but after many years, she finally left me. It was my fault, not hers. We have two children.

"For the past two years, I've been a bum. I left Oregon and hitch-hiked to Nevada on my way to Arizona and the house in Phoenix. I want my wife and kids back."

"How old are you?"

He gave me his age. To my surprise, he was younger than me. His beard was white. His name was Mike.

"Would you come with me into the church again?" I asked. "I want to get the elders and the pastor you spoke with this morning. I want them to explain why they couldn't help you with money or send someone to McDonald's with you. Will you do that with me?"

"Yes."

We walked in and found many people still there. Mike pointed out the pastor, who turned out to be the senior pastor, and two elders. I asked to speak with them. Mike stood to my right.

I related Mike's story and asked, "Is that right?"

All three lowered their heads and said, "Yes."

Finally, the senior pastor told the elder who also served as office manager, "Go write out a check for twenty dollars payable to Albertsons and write 'no alcohol' on it."

I waited with Mike. No one moved or spoke. The elder came back with the check and gave it to Mike, who put it in his shirt pocket.

As we walked to McDonald's, I felt proud of Mike. *He told the truth*, I thought. "Can I look at the check?"

I was shocked to find it was only for ten dollars. "How much was this supposed to be?"

"They said twenty bucks."

I toyed with the idea of going back then decided against it.

At McDonald's, Mike bought three hamburgers, two orders of French fries, and a drink. Later, we stopped at the supermarket for food for his trip to Phoenix. I drove him to the Arizona border. We talked for a while, then I gave him what little money I had and drove off. I looked in the rearview mirror and saw him standing there, watching me go, and I began to cry.

Lord willing, Mike, I thought, *I'll see you in heaven.*

And Jesus spoke, "For I was hungry and you gave Me no food; I was thirsty and you gave Me no drink" (Matthew 25:42). James 2:1–13 is also very important in relation to Mike. It discusses showing, during church, favoritism to the well-to-do at the expense of the poor.

Chapter Twenty
The Wolves Howl

Several years ago, I attended a church for fellowship with the body of Christ. Soon after, I heard God speak to me about the pastor.

This man wears his humility on his sleeve for everyone to see. He's filled with pride inside.

God opened my eyes to the man's self-serving ministry. His motives were deceptive. Many people came to me in excitement and asked, "Isn't this great?" I smiled. I'll call the man Paul.

When the opportunity came, Paul fired his assistant pastor to make room for another who would bring more people into the church. I'll call the second man Joe. Joe had been the morning host of the only Christian radio station in town. The assistant pastor wasn't flashy; he was a man with a good heart who wanted to serve the Lord. The senior pastor seemed to know I was aware of his egotistic, self-serving ministry, although I didn't say a word to anyone.

I had to stop attending. I couldn't bear to see people used for another man's ego, all in the name of Jesus.

Four years passed. Then I heard there was a split within the church. At the time of the split, it was the largest church in Nevada, featured on national television as one of the fastest-growing megachurches in America. Someone told me that two assistant pastors broke from the senior pastor, because he was, as they said, "dictatorial and in it for what he could get."

I decided to attend one of their home Bible fellowships. I enjoyed the meeting, and after it was over, I was invited to the church, located in a shopping center.

I attended for a few weeks, then one Sunday night, the pastor's wife asked me, "Rene, would you like to go with the pastors and elders? They're going near the other church to pray."

I agreed.

A large van was in the parking lot for us. The pastor drove. I sat in the back of a group of eleven. When we arrived, we parked across the street in a supermarket parking lot.

Then they began to pray.

"O Lord, they said they're right, and the whole town will bow before them. Lord, show them that Paul is only interested in his own welfare."

"They prophesied our destruction," someone added.

I was disturbed about that and sought God.

"Go inside the church," Jesus told me. "You 'll see one of the two pastors. Tell him he must repent and step down. If he does so willingly, I'll keep it quiet. If he tries to cover it up, I'll publicly expose him."

I told the others what God told me. No one spoke for a moment. When I started to leave, one said, "Paul and Joe are both gone by now. It's ten thirty. They never stay this late."

"I heard God's voice. One of them is inside."

I walked across the road into the church's parking lot. *Maybe they won't believe me when I tell them what happened*, I thought. *I'll ask one of them to come with me.*

I went back to the van and asked if someone would come with me. No one moved or spoke.

"The person doesn't have to say a word, just watch," I added.

"Okay," someone said. "I'll come."

As we approached the church, he got nervous. "What are you going to say? What will you do?" His steps slowed, and he lagged behind.

"Just listen," I said.

I entered the church and saw three or four couples in the large room the church used for meetings. I'd never been there before when it was a church, just when it was a supermarket. A man stood in the middle of the room with one man inside the sound booth and another leaning over, talking to him. I guessed their wives were nearby.

I walked up to the man leaning over. "Is one of the pastors here?"

He looked startled. "What for?"

"I want to talk to him."

"I'm Joe. I'm one of the pastors."

I never saw him before, but I heard his voice when he hosted the radio program. We moved a few feet away from the women. The man who came with me from the van looked ready to faint.

I told him what God told me to say. Joe was very polite about it and listened carefully.

"I'll pray over it," he said finally. "What's your name?"

I told him, shook his hand, and left.

When we got back to the van, my companion was excited and told everyone what happened. They seemed happy.

One month later, an exposé of Joe appeared on the front page of the local newspaper. He'd been caught having an affair with a woman disc jockey who attended his church. They used church money to visit San Diego and other places. It was a very sordid situation.

Joe left the church and, six months later, started another one. I waited for two years before approaching him again.

One Wednesday night, I visited him. He didn't recognize me until I mentioned my name.

"Rene? You're the one! I've thought of you often. I should've listened to you."

We had a friendly conversation. He said he repented. I never saw him again. Eighteen months later, Joe divorced his wife and moved to Los Angeles to make a career as a secular songwriter and musician.

My heart cries. Why doesn't the church receive correction? When will the leaders truly trust in the living God and draw near to Him? They howl like wolves and roar like lions. They pollute God's church with insolent, deceitful tongues. O Lord, restore to your church a pure tongue, that we may serve You with one accord. Deliver us from the hawkers who emit the loud, long howls of self-appointed professional wolves.

May we be clothed inwardly with Christ's virtues and consolations as we partake from the holy grail of the cross, His body and blood. To God be the glory through His Son forever.

Today, I asked the Lord, "What's the meaning of 'taking up my cross and following You'?"

He replied, "My son, mortify all selfish desires within your flesh as the image of My stigmata is placed within your heart."

The days of God's grace are coming to an end. Unity between God's remnant church and the larger apostate church are also coming to an end.

God … always God.

Chapter Twenty-One
Where Does God Really Dwell?

Where does God really dwell? He dwells in the one who is poor and of a contrite spirit (Isaiah 66:2). He is near those who have a broken heart and truly accepts the sacrifices of one who has a broken spirit (Psalm 51:17). He hides them under the shadow of His wings (Psalm 17:8), and they dwell in the secret place of the Most high, abiding under the shadow of the Almighty (Psalm 91:1).

Sometimes, the truth divides. It has to, to separate truth from error. Jesus asked, "Do you suppose that I came to give peace on earth? I tell you, not at all, but rather division" (Luke 12:51).

Do not be afraid of those who would label you as one who causes division, if it's truly for the cause of Christ. Only a few of those who are seekers of the narrow gate will be saved (Luke 13:24). Jesus was never impressed by those with high and great reputations. The religious leaders said to Him, "Nor do you care about anyone, for you do not regard the person of men" (Matthew 22:16).

If you really want to work for God, simply believe in Jesus (John 6:28–29). He'll take care of the rest. May they say of us, "They are full of new wine" (Acts 2:13), not realizing, in their self-righteousness, what they're saying—new wine is revival.

Chapter Twenty-Two
Hypocrisy in the Church

Hypocrisy in the church is a showy, empty display of religion. Hypocrisy in religion manifests in display, formalism, and ceremonialism. It's worldly, legalistic, and satanic. Those who get involved in it become self-righteous, superficially impressive, blind, and worst of all, bound in men's traditions.

They pretend to be holy, but inwardly, they'll be filled with themselves. Everything they do is for outward appearance, and they love their titles. Sometimes, they give half-truths, which are, in the end, lies. The saddest thing that hypocrisy brings is apostasy and a theatrical presentation.

Chapter Twenty-Three
Revolution for the Church

The problem isn't that the church is in the world; it's that the world is in the church. We, as Christians, are to lead the world to Christ. All too often, we imitate the world's lead. Whatever the world has or does, we do the same, and we add Christ to it.

We are commanded to be holy (1 Peter 1:15–16). *Holy* means that we're to be different and set apart, not the same. All too often, our meetings are social clubs with Jesus added. Something has happened in the last twenty years—young pastors are locating themselves in shopping centers. Shopping-center Christianity is something where people add Jesus to a worldly lifestyle. Everything is convenient—we pick God's gift off the shelf whenever we want.

A pastor is supposed to be an elder, which means an aged or older person. Young people are to submit to them (1 Peter 5:1–5). Quickly, they ask, "How about Timothy?" Paul never said he was an elder at that time. As a result, we've become friends with the world, not knowing we were at enmity with God (James 4:4). We can recognize it by knowing that where there is envy and self-seeking, every evil thing will be there too (James 3:16).

The church started in people's homes. The Bible clearly shows how small groups met in private homes (1 Corinthians 16:19, Romans 16:5, Colossians 4:15). In the end, the church must go back to homes. All too often, men have built towers of Babel to their egos. God doesn't live in temples made by men's hands. The only temple He's interested in is our body. The Lord's house is us, not buildings. Those are just places where we meet.

Men love their titles of honor and love to be called Reverend. In the Bible, *Reverend* is used only once and then only for God.

> Holy and Reverend [awesome] is His name. (Psalm 111:9, King James Version)

Why would men use that term? It's God's name.

We must be aware of the traditions of men. What we have now is, largely, no longer Christian. It's two thousand years' worth of what men said Christianity should be. Centuries after God gave His Word to Moses, God had to do a new thing (Matthew 23). Men had corrupted God's Word so much He had to move away from their corruption. During the last two thousand years, men again corrupted God's pure Word.

When Jesus was on earth, people didn't recognize Him. They were Word people, people who trusted the Bible, but they wouldn't accept Jesus.

We are Moses's disciples; we know God spoke to Moses. As for this fellow (Jesus), we do not know where He is from (John 9:28–29).

They trusted their interpretation of the Word, and He, the Word, was before them. The people believed in Him, but some of those who studied the Bible didn't.

Have any of the rulers or Pharisees believed in Him? But this crowd that does not know the law is accursed (John 7:48–49).

Sometimes, knowledge of scripture makes one arrogant (1 Corinthians 8:1), but love always edifies.

In heaven, God balances everything in harmony. Men haven't balanced scripture with scripture. That's one reason the body of Christ doesn't have the power it once had.

> You have been weighed in the balances and found wanting (Daniel 5:27).

I wrote this book in the hope that the church will once again be balanced before Christ's return.

Chapter Twenty-Four
Corruption in the Church

Did Jesus Christ establish a denomination? The early church had no form of human organization—the believers simply considered themselves one in Christ. The church of Christ should have no humanly controlled organization, just divine fellowship. The church of Jesus cannot and should not have a human head.

Jesus Christ alone is the head of the Christian church (Ephesians 1:22–23). Men love to be the head of things, little kings of their own little kingdoms. Mostly, they say, "Allegiance to this church. Be faithful to this movement."

It takes a lot of work to hold together such a human organization and assembly. God, by His spirit, builds His church. Men need only follow. The human mind regulates the human body. When men lose their mind, they become insane, and others dominate them. The body of Christ—the church—should have the mind of Christ and be ruled by Him.

The problem, after two thousand years of men's traditions, is that the body of Christ all too often has too many small babbling human heads, bringing confusion and sickness to the body. Sometimes, it seems insane. That's why many parts of the church commit spiritual adultery. It all too often has a human head and unknowingly rejects its true husband, Jesus Christ (Ephesians 5:23–24).

Many theologians have written extensively about Mystery, Babylon the Great, the mother of harlots and of the abominations of the earth (Revelations 17:5). They have identified her as a large religious system that covers the earth, which is corrupt. The focus is always on her.

I have a question: If she is the corrupted huge religious system that fills the earth, she has daughters, and they are the harlots. Who are the daughters? What has come from this large religious system? The daughters point the finger at the mother and say, "How corrupt you are." They don't realize that when they point one finger, three more in their hands point right back at them.

If she could only be made to realize her pathetic condition, there might be some chance for repentance. They can't see because they're blinded by the building of massive structures and organizations seeking recognition and wealth in the world, building monuments to men's egos.

"They do not know that they are wretched, miserable, poor, blind, and naked" (Revelations 3:17).

Why are they blind to their real condition? Because they are self-deceived, thinking they are rich, having become wealthy, and having need of nothing (Revelations 3:17).

She thinks she is rich and prosperous, increasing in numbers. What should we do?

"Come out of her, my people, lest you share in her sins, and lest you receive of her plagues" (Revelations 18:4).

Some say, "Yes, I see now. I'll change her from within."

"Listen to God," I reply.

Chapter Twenty-Five

The Unholy Marriage

Temptation comes to us in times of weakness and strength. When our desires unite (have spiritual intercourse) with temptation, an unholy union takes place. The tempter plants his seed in our desires, and we become pregnant with his sin. After a while, the fetus grows, and we give birth to the child, whose name is sin.

The creature will grow, and when he is full-grown, he brings a surprise he hid from you—death.

Do not focus on sin; that only gives it strength. Focus on Jesus. If you say yes to Jesus, you won't have to say no to sin. Sin doesn't satisfy. Many have given themselves over to sin, thinking it will satisfy. Sin, when practiced, only creates the desire for more. It's addictive.

If one shows mercy to sin, one day, sin will have grown strong and won't show mercy to you. Put it to death, or it will do the same to you. God and sin both want you—you must choose. Recognize your nothingness and that God is all, and that will help you decide.

Prophecy, vision, dreams, and thoughts were given to Rene Bates relating to the end times. The day and hour weren't given. Man's calendar could be incorrect a few years, but God's calendar is correct. Our calendar is based on when Jesus Christ was born, but no one knows the exact year.

Chapter Twenty-Six
His Coming Is Near

Many will say, "No one knows the day and hour of the Lord's return" (Matthew 24:36). But the Lord hasn't given the day and hour. He didn't say he wouldn't give the year, month, or week. Sometimes, God speaks loudly by what He doesn't say.

Three verses previous, He says, "We are to know when it is near, at the very doors" (Matthew 24:33).

Peter wrote, "The end of all things is at hand" (1 Peter 4:7). John wrote, "It is the last hour" (1 John 2:18). Paul wrote, "We are not in darkness, so that this day should overtake us as a thief, meaning the day of the Lord" (1 Thessalonians 5:4). James wrote, "The coming of the Lord is at hand" (James 5:8).

It's clear that if nothing else, we'll have an inner witness that the end is near. There will be those who scoff in the last days, asking, "Where is the promise of His coming? Things have always been like this since the beginning of creation" (2 Peter 3:4).

When they scoff and mock in that way, that is a sign of Christ's imminent return.

Discern the time.

"As you see the day drawing near" (Hebrews 10:25).

"For salvation ready to be revealed in the last time" (1 Peter 1:5).

"The revelation of Jesus Christ, which God gave Him to show His servants—things which must shortly take place" (Revelation 1:1).

"But if that evil servant says in his heart, 'My Master is delaying his coming'" (Matthew 24:48).

Chapter Twenty-Seven
The Last Ten Years Chronologically

Tenth year—A year of thanks.

Ninth Year—The Lord will perfect His remnant and separate them from the wicked.

Eighth Year—God's people will just begin to feel afflicted, troubled, and distressed as the appointed time nears. The time is approaching. He shall build up and make strong a people.

Seventh Year—The Lord's tender mercies comfort His people. He pities them and has compassion on them. It's time to heed the voice of His Word.

Sixth Year—Time for His people to praise Him. His ministers are very bold and strong. Earthquakes and volcanoes are terrible. Many wicked are consumed, but God's people praise Him.

Fifth Year—A time of great evangelism. God's people proclaim His glory. God's judgments are in the earth. The beginning of famine. The fish in the waters are polluted. Much hail on the earth. Fire is abundant. Vegetation is struck down by God. Many babies die. God separates His people. He takes care of them. People want to harm His prophets.

Fourth Year—God's people praise Him because He has forgiven them all their sins. They have joy and happiness in this. They prepare for their inheritance. A plague breaks out on the earth. God's wrath is kindled.

Third Year—God redeems His people. He delivers them out of trouble and distress. They go to a city of habitation. He brings them out of the shadow of death and darkness. He calms the storm for them. He guides them.

Second Year—God's people begin to see victory over the enemy. Only God can help his people.

The year before the Lord returns—God's judgment on the wicked.

The year of our Lord's return—Messiah Jesus reigns. His power is beautiful in holiness. Judgment among the nations. The body and head are united.

Chapter Twenty-Eight
The Vision of the Body and Head Uniting

One week later, I received the following vision of how the body and head will unite.

I saw the body of Christ, and it was weak and sickly. Two feet above the neck, but not connected to it, was the head. As I looked closer, I saw tiny heads with open mouths coming out of the neck. There were thousands of them, all babbling loudly, bringing confusion and disorder to the body. No one listened.

Then I heard God in heaven say, "I shall send forth my angels from heaven, and they shall uproot these babblers."

Angels came down and plucked the small babbling heads until the last one was gone. The body seemed stronger, and for a moment, there was silence. Then slowly, the head came down to the neck.

"There is only one head for My body."

I waited.

Next, I saw a hand with a burning match move closer to the feet of the body. The toes caught fire, and the flame rose up the body. Some parts burned more than others, but all were purged by the fire. It burned to the neck, where the babbling heads had been, but it stopped below the head of Jesus Christ.

"The vision is true. Go tell your brothers."

A time of purging, baptizing fire is coming. Praise be to God.

All is apostate to one degree or another. Only God can remove from the body what needs to be taken out. A dream followed my vision.

I was walking, and people said, "Come! See the master. Come see Jesus!"

They had ugly scars on their bodies. "Before you can see Him, you have to come with us. There are things that must be removed from everyone."

God showed me that only He can remove what needs to be taken from the body. If men try, they will only scar themselves.

Men have used God, His name, and His word for personal gain. He will end that gradually. We must turn away from man-centered religion that only glorifies man. They preach an entertainment gospel.

> Not everyone who says to Me "Lord, Lord" shall enter the kingdom of heaven, but he who does the will of My Father in heaven. Many will say to Me in that day, "Lord, Lord, have we not prophesied in Your name, cast out demons in Your name, and done many wonders [works] in Your name?"
>
> And then I will declare to them, "I never knew you. Depart from Me, you who practice lawlessness." (Matthew 7:21–28)

Some modern religious leaders do all three things, but God arranges in the body whoever He wants. The rebellion is that men always want to move higher. They aren't content with being a kneecap. They want to be the head. They want to be something great. They want to be a member who is presentable, someone who's noticed.

But now God has set the members, each one of them in the body just as He pleased. And if they were all one member, where would the body be? But now, indeed, there are many members, yet one body, and the eye cannot say to the hand, "I have no need of you," or again, the head to the feet, "I have no need of you."

No, much rather, those members of the body who seem to be weaker are necessary, and those members of the body whom we think to be less honorable on these, we bestow greater honor, and our unpresentable parts have greater modesty. But our presentable parts have no need, but God composed the body, having given greater honor to the part that lacks it, that there should be no schism, but that the members should have the same care one for another (1 Corinthians 12:18–25).

It seems that the greatest hindrance for the headship of the Lord Jesus Christ over His body is the man-made Christian religious system, with its clergy, causing a division in the body of Christ. That clergy-laity division was something Jesus said should not be. Read Matthew 23:8–9, Matthew 20:25–28, and Revelations 2:6. The word *clergy* isn't in the New Testament.

God will teach man a hard lesson. He chooses whom He wants. In Matthew 20, there is a parable of the workers in the vineyards. Some worked all day, some worked from noon until quitting time in the afternoon, and some worked only half an hour. He paid the last ones first. The ones who worked only half an hour got a certain amount of money, and those who worked all day expected to get more, but they were paid the same.

> Take what is yours and go your way. I wish to give to this last man the same as to you. Is it not lawful for me to do what I wish with my own things? Or is your eye evil, because I am good? So, the last will be first, and the first will be last. For many are called, but few are chosen. (Matthew 20:14–16)

Many think that by working long and hard, they'll be greater in God's kingdom. There, the last will be first, and the first will be last. God does the choosing.

For He says to Moses, "I will have mercy on whomever I will have mercy, and I will have compassion on whomever I will have compassion. So then it is not of him who wills, nor of him who runs, but of God who shows mercy."

For the scriptures say to Pharaoh, "Even for this same purpose I raised you up, that I might show My power in you and that My name might be declared in all the earth."

Therefore, He has mercy on whom He wills, and whom He wills, He hardens (Romans 9:15–17).

Chapter Twenty-Nine
Nicolaitans

"But this you have, that you hate the deeds of the Nicolaitans, which I also hate" (Revelations 2:6). Dividing the church between clergy and laity.

> Jesus said, "You know that the rulers of the Gentiles lorded over them, and those who are great exercise authority over them. Yet it should not be so among you. But whoever desires to become great among you, let him be your servant, and whoever desires to be first among you, let him be your slave, just as the son of man didn't come to be served, but to serve and to give His life as ransom for many." (Matthew 20:25–28)
>
> But all their works they do to be seen by men. They make their phylacteries broad and enlarge the borders of their garments. They love the best places at feasts, the best seats in the synagogues, greetings in the marketplaces, and to be called by men, "Rabbi, Rabbi."
>
> But you do not be called Rabbi, for One is your Teacher, the Christ, and you are all brethren. Do not call anyone on earth your father; for One is your Father, He who is in heaven. And do not be called teachers; for One is your Teacher, the Christ. But he who is greatest among you shall be your servant. And whoever exalts himself

> will be abased, and he who humbles himself will be exalted. (Matthew 23:5–12)

Men's titles in His body are an offense to God. The division between clergy and laity will be purged. No one is called by a title before their name in God's church except Lord Jesus Christ in the New Testament. There is a difference between having an office in the church and being called by that office.

Nico in Greek means "lording over someone," "a victory over the people." *Laitians* means "the laity." *Minister* means "servant," "one who must serve and who is an example to the flock," "the one who does menial jobs." *Rabbi* means "master" and is a title of honor.

Jesus clearly said to call no one by a title of honor. He never did. We have the fivefold ministry offices, but we aren't to elevate them with titles. Paul was Paul; Peter was Peter. They had the office, but they weren't called by it.

In the above scripture, Jesus condemned the calling of titles before names, including appellations of honor in His church.

Chapter Thirty
God's Holy Flame

The fire will purge the body from two fatal sins—perversion, both physical and spiritual, and worldliness or adultery. Spiritual perversion has its roots in self-love. Fig-leaf Christians are those who cover themselves with their self-righteousness. Some Christians who don't fear God seek Him only for what they can get out of Him. They love themselves more than God. That isn't true communication with God. They are revealed in Luke 18:9–14 in the parable of the Pharisee and the tax collector.

"For all seek their own, not the things which are of Christ Jesus" (Phil. 2:21).

Spiritual perversion is also manifested in homogeneous spirituality. By that I mean those who love their own kind, trying to make everyone like themselves in praise and thinking. Many look to their own way for gain, creating a wasteland and much desolation.

All you beasts of the field, come to devour
All you beasts in the forest.
His watchmen are blind,
They are all ignorant,
They are all dumb dogs,
They cannot bark;
Sleeping, lying down,
Loving to slumber.
Yes, they are greedy dogs
Which never have enough
And they are shepherds [pastors]

Who cannot understand;
They all look to their own way,
Every one for his own gain,
From his own territory [church]
"Come," one says, "I will bring wine,
And we will fill ourselves with intoxicating drink;
Tomorrow will be as today,
And much more abundant [prosperous]."
(Isaiah 56:9–12)

It's shameful how some hock their wares and peddle their trinkets to the people. Why doesn't Jesus do in their ministry what He did in His?

Her heads judge for a bribe,
Her priests teach for pay,
And her prophets divine for money.
Yet they lean on the Lord, and say,
"Is not the Lord among us?
No harm can come upon us" [self-deception].
(Micah 3:11)

There is no true repose for the soul until it finds its rest in God. Once there, the soul works without ceasing, never tiring, because it's God who is working in us. Works of the flesh burn out, but being yoked with Jesus strengthens and purifies us.

Chapter Thirty-One
Soul Power

The wolf is the devil, the thief is the hireling.
—John 10:10–13

The fire will also purge worldliness from the body. All the hirelings will be purged—the hireling pastors, leaders, and entertainers—those who do what they do for pay. I wonder how many would do those things if they weren't being paid. Those are the ones who know how to rally crowds and how to communicate in the realm of the soul. God's realm is spirit, and He uses His Holy Spirit to transmit to man's spirit. The soul is man's emotions, desires, and wants. Men's souls can only touch other men's souls. If something isn't done by the Holy Spirit, it has no eternal value.

The soul copies everything the spirit can do, producing fake worship, deceitful salvation, and counterfeit revival. When men use their souls, they can only transmit to other souls. God, through His Holy Spirit, imparts to men's spirits. When men use their souls and connect with other men's souls, they're only worshipping themselves—no matter what they say. To worship themselves is indirectly worshipping Satan. Men's souls are the gateway to Satan, but the power of the Holy Spirit is beyond men's control. The power of the soul makes people weep and is controlled by men.

There are defects in the church today. Believers are instructed in nothing more than expounding scriptures. Their knowledge of scripture is good, but they don't have a deeper growth in the spiritual life. They have narrow spirits and broad heads. Today, people feel warm and joyful when they go to church, because everything is aimed at their souls to make them feel good. They should be convicted and want to repent. Most preaching today simply helps the mind. Whatever is done in the spirit can be duplicated by the soul.

Men are fooled by what other men say or do. It doesn't matter what men say; it only matters what God says. Men's desire to play it safe is recklessness in God's kingdom. They don't really want to take a chance on God. Their meetings are controlled, stifling the spirit. God looks into men's hearts. Lusting after recognition and position will be judged. Many steal from one another and from God.

> An astonishing and horrible thing has been committed in the land. The prophets prophesied falsely, and the priests ruled by their own power, and my people loved to have it so. But what will you do at the end of it? (Jeremiah 5:30–31)

Many have called themselves to the ministry.

And the Lord said to me, "The Prophets prophesied lies in My name. I have not sent them, commanded them, nor spoken to them. They prophesy to you a false vision divination, a worthless thing the deceit of their own heart (Jeremiah 14:14).

"I have not sent these prophets, yet they ran. I have not spoken to them, yet they prophesy. Is not My word like fire," says the Lord, "and like a hammer that breaks a rock in pieces? Therefore, behold, I am against these prophets, who steal My word everyone from his neighbor" (Jeremiah 23:20–21, 29–30).

Many have called themselves, but God hasn't called them. They are self-appointed, not God-anointed. Through the Bible, they steal from Him, saying, "God has said." They try to control His written word for their benefit.

Then He spoke a parable to them: "No one puts a piece from a new garment on an old one; otherwise, the new makes a tear, and also the piece that was taken out of the new does not match the old. And no one puts new wine into old wineskins; or else the new wine will burst the wineskins and be spilled, and the wineskins will be ruined. But new wine must be put into new wineskins, and both are preserved. And no one, having drunk old wine, immediately desires new; for he says, 'The old is better'" (Luke 5:36–39).

God will do a new thing. He will put new wine (His Spirit) into new wineskins (people). The old wineskins (organized religion) won't accept the new wine. Religious leaders resisted Jesus, but God was doing a new thing. They said the old way was better. God is always moving forward, which is why He seldom uses an old way.

"Now when they saw the boldness of Peter and John, and perceived they were uneducated and untrained men, they marveled. And they realized that they had been with Jesus" (Acts 4:13).

God has a principle—he usually uses untrained, uneducated men, but they've been with Jesus. Today, men reverse the process. Many seek to be educated and highly trained, but many haven't been with Jesus. They even accused Jesus of not studying the Bible. Please read John 7:15.

It's time to examine our hearts for the motives behind what we say and do for Jesus. Our Lord is merciful and gracious and gives us time to repent. False peace is putting people to sleep—behind it is much violence. God's judgment isn't far away. Now is the time to turn our hearts to God. Many no longer fear God, but they will. The Lord told me that if they'd fear Him, it would keep them from much sin. Remember what Jesus said in Matthew 10:28.

"And do not fear those who kill the body but cannot kill the soul. But rather fear Him who is able to destroy both soul and body in hell" (Matthew 10:28).

Fear means "awe" and "respect" as well as "to frighten or be alarmed."

> And the Lord God of their fathers sent warning to them by His messengers, rising up early and sending them because He had compassion on His people and on His dwelling place. But they mocked the messengers of God, despised His words, and scoffed at His prophets, until the wrath of the Lord arose against His people, until there was no remedy. (1 Chronicles 36:15–16)

> You search the Scriptures [Bible] for in them you think you have eternal life; and these are they which testify to Me. But you are not willing to come to Me that you may have life. I do not receive honor from men. But I know you, that you do not have the love of God in you. I have come in My Father's name, and you do not receive Me; if another comes in his own name, him you will receive. How can you believe, who receive honor from one another, and do not seek the honor that comes from the only God? (John 5:39–44)

The false church looks godly but is corrupt in the last days.

> In the last days, perilous times will come. Men will be lovers of themselves, lovers of money, boastful, proud, blasphemers, disobedient to parents, unthankful, unholy, unloving, un-forgiving, slanderous, without self-control, brutal, despisers of good, traitors, headstrong, haughty, lovers of pleasure rather than lovers of God, having a form of godliness but denying its power. And from such people, turn away. (2 Timothy 3:1–5)

They look like Christians, but they don't have any real power—power from God. That's why they deny it.

I want you to understand that this is meant for the leadership of today. God has a chapter for pastors in the Bible. Like all scripture, it speaks for itself. It was religious leaders, those who taught the Bible and were proud of their positions, who condemned Jesus to death (Mark 10:33–34). Jesus also warned us to beware of their teaching (Matthew 16:5–12). Watch how some will attack me. They want the light put everywhere except on themselves (John 3:19–21). The light would expose their motives. Let God's light shine forth on all. Pretenders love to hide behind a veneer of respectability.

In the following scripture, the shepherds of Israel are the pastors of God's people.

> And the word of the Lord came to me, saying, "Son of man, prophesy against the shepherds of Israel, prophesy and say to them, 'Thus says the Lord God to the shepherds of Israel who feed themselves—should not the shepherds feed the flocks? You eat the fat and clothe yourselves with the wool; you slaughter the fatlings but you do not feed the flock. The weak you have not strengthened nor have you healed those who were sick nor bound up the broken nor brought back what was driven away nor sought what was lost.
>
> "'With force and cruelty, you have ruled them. So, they were scattered because there was no [real] shepherd, and they became food for all the beasts of the field [demons] when they were scattered.'
>
> "My sheep [Christians] wandered through all the mountains and every high hill. Yes, my flock was scattered over the whole face of the earth, and no one was seeking or searching. Therefore, you shepherds hear the word of the Lord.
>
> "'As I live,' says the Lord God, 'surely because my flock became a prey, and my flock became food for every beast of the field because there was no shepherd, nor did my shepherds search for my flock, but the shepherds fed themselves and did not feed my flock. Therefore, oh, shepherds, hear the word of the Lord.
>
> "'Behold, I am against the shepherds. I will require my flock at their hand. I will cause them to cease feeding the sheep, and the shepherds shall feed themselves no more, for I will deliver my flock from their mouths that they may no longer be food for them.'

"For thus says the Lord God, 'Indeed, I myself will search for my sheep and seek them out, as a shepherd seeks out his flock on the day he is among his scattered sheep, so will I seek out my sheep and deliver them from all the places where they were scattered on a cloudy, dark day, and I will bring them out from the peoples and gather them from the countries, and I will bring them to their own land. I will feed them on the mountains of Israel, in the valleys and all the inhabited places of the country.

"'I will feed them in good pasture, and their fold shall be on the high mountains of Israel. There they shall lie down in a good fold and feed in rich pastures on the mountains of Israel. I will feed my flock, and I will make them lie down. I will seek what was lost and bring back what was driven away, bind up the broken and strengthen the sick, but I will destroy the fat and the strong and feed them in judgment.

"'And as for you, oh, my flock,' says the Lord God, 'behold, I will judge between sheep and sheep, between rams and goats. Is it too little for you to have eaten up the good pasture that you must tread down with your feet the residue of your pasture? And to have drunk on the clear waters that you must foul the residue with your feet? And as for my flock, they eat what you have trampled with your feet, and they drink what you have fouled with your feet.

"'Therefore,' says the Lord God to them, 'behold, I, myself, will judge between the fat and the lean sheep. Because you have pushed with side and shoulder, butted the weak and scattered them abroad, therefore, I will save My flock, and they shall no longer be a prey, and I will judge

> between sheep and sheep. I will establish one shepherd over them, and he shall feed them, my servant David [Jesus Christ], and he shall feed them and become their shepherd, and I, the Lord, will be their God, and my servant David a prince among them.
>
> "'I, the Lord, have spoken. I will make a covenant of peace with them and cause the wild beast to cease from the land, and they will dwell safely in the wilderness and sleep in the woods. I will make them in the places all around My hill a blessing, and I will cause showers to come down in their seasons, and they will be showers of blessings.
>
> "'The trees in the fields shall yield their fruit, and the earth shall yield their increase. They shall be safe in their land, and they shall know that I am the Lord when I have broken the bonds of their yoke and delivered them from the land of those who enslaved them, and they shall no longer be a prey for the nations, nor shall the beast of the land devour them.
>
> "'But they shall dwell in safety, and no one shall make them afraid. I'll raise up for them a garden of renown, and they shall no longer be consumed with hunger in the land nor bear the shame of the Gentiles anymore. Thus, they shall know that I, the Lord their God, am with them, and that they, the House of Israel, are my people,' says the Lord God. 'You are my flock, the flock of my pasture. You are men, and I am your God.'" (Ezekiel 34)

Who are the hireling shepherds and professional pastors in the last days? God tells us.

> Nor did we eat anyone's bread free of charge but worked with labor and toiled night and day, that we might not be a burden to any of you, not because we do not have authority, but to make ourselves an example of how you should follow us. (2 Thessalonians 3:8–9)
>
> For you remember, brethren, our labor and toil for laboring night and day that we might not be a burden to any of you. We preach to you the gospel of God. (1 Thessalonians 2:9)

The following scripture was written to the elders and overseers of the church:

> I have coveted no one's silver or gold or apparel. Yes, you yourselves, know that these hands have provided for those necessities and, for those who were with me, I have shown you in every way, in laboring like this, that you must support the weak and remember the words of our Lord Jesus Christ, that He said, "It is more blessed to give than to receive." (Acts 20:33–35)
>
> What is my reward then? That when I preach the gospel, I may present the gospel of Christ without charge that I may not abuse my authority in the gospel. (1 Corinthians 9:18)

Why are not these scriptures ever preached?

> Freely you have received, freely give. (Matthew 10:8)
>
> Men of corrupt minds and destitute of the truth, who suppose that godliness is a means of gain. From such withdraw yourself. (1 Timothy 6:5)

> And we labor, working with our own hands. (1 Corinthians 4:12)
>
> And to work with your own hands, as we commanded you. (1 Thessalonians 4:11)
>
> For now, the third time, I am ready to come to you. And I will not be burdensome to you, for I do not seek yours but you. For the children are not to lay up for the parents, but the parents for the children. And I will very gladly spend and be spent for your souls, though the more abundantly I love you, the less I am loved. For be that as it may—I did not burden you, nevertheless being crafty. I caught you with guile. Did I take advantage of you by any of those that I sent to you? (2 Corinthians 12:14–17)
>
> For we are not as so many, peddling the word of God. (2 Corinthians 2:17)
>
> For all seek their own, not the things which are of Christ Jesus. (Philippians 2:21)

Many have taken financial advantage of people. There are very few who should receive a wage. Most should be an example to the people as the early church elders were. Money was collected, but it was to be given to the poor, not for huge salaries. The money was not to be pressured out of people, but only as God proposed it in their hearts.

Religious leaders had Jesus crucified because they feared losing their positions of honor. They said, "If we let Him alone like this, everyone will believe in Him, and the Romans will come and take away both our place and nation" (John 11:48).

Has anything really changed? Read Mark 10:21, Romans 15:26, 1 Corinthians 16:1–2, 2 Corinthians 8:14, and 2 Corinthians 9:7. There is also the Laodicean church:

"That they are rich and have become wealthy and have need of nothing, they do not know they are wretched, miserable, poor, blind, and naked" (Revelations 3).

Jesus counsels them to buy gold from him, but what is this gold but those who have been refined in the fire? They will not do so.

> Woe to you scribes and Pharisees [separated ones] you hypocrites, for you cleanse the outside of the cup and dish, but inside, they are lull of extortion and self-indulgence. Blind Pharisee, first cleanse the inside of the cup and dish, that the outside of them may be clean also.
>
> Woe to you scribes and Pharisees, for you are like whitewashed tombs which indeed appear beautiful outwardly, but inside are full of dead men's bones and all uncleanliness. Even so, you outwardly appear righteous to men, but inside, you are full of hypocrisy and lawlessness. (Matthew 23:25–28)

In Matthew 24:4–5, Jesus warned us of false Christs and false prophets. The false Christs are the false anointings—*Christ* means "anointed." The false prophets are the ones who claim to speak for God but who are false. They will rise and show great signs, but we aren't to listen to them. Deception will be rampant.

The first sign of the end is deception from false Christs. Many coming in Jesus's name saying "Jesus is the Christ" will deceive many, not to mention the merchandisers in the temple and how Jesus drove them out, saying, "My Father's house is a house of prayer" (Matthew 11:15–17). He drove out those who do business in the Lord's house.

One of the reasons there is no power in the church is because people don't recognize the authority in God's church, the authority that God Himself placed there. They are not entertainers but willing to be nothing. That is God's order in His church.

"And God has appointed these in the church, first Apostles, second prophets, third teachers, after that miracles, then gifts of healing, helps, administrations, varieties of tongues" (1 Corinthians 12:28).

God said first the Apostles, then the prophets, and then the teachers. Why are they linked in succession? Because He wants order, submission, and authority in His church—balance. Today, pastors are exalted to the quenching of other ministries.

"And He Himself gave some to be Apostles, some prophets, some evangelists, some pastors, and teachers" (Ephesians 4:11).

One office and gift balances the others. Focusing on one gift (teaching) and one office (the pastor) quenches the other gifts and brings big heads and narrow spirits to the body. Head knowledge sometimes brings pride, and without the other gifts, the body becomes unbalanced.

Jesus told us how to have church in 1 Corinthians 14:37. He wants the whole body used, not just one or two parts. Please read 1 Corinthians 14:26–40.

The order in a church meeting is to "let two or three prophets speak" (1 Corinthians 14:29). It seems that leaders today have great difficulty with that. "If something is revealed to one who is seated, he should be allowed freedom to speak and not be quenched" (1 Corinthians 14:30). Those truly in leadership would be very grieved by that.

"Obey those who rule over you, and be submissive, for they watch out for your souls as those who must give an account. Let them do so with joy and not with grief, for that would be unprofitable to you" (Hebrews 13:17).

In Mark 15:10, religious leaders handed Jesus over to the authorities out of envy. They didn't want to release their power. Today, much of Christian leadership isn't in God's order.

Jesus teaches the same thing beginning in Matthew 8:5.

> Now when Jesus entered Capernaum, a centurion came to Him, pleading with Him, saying, "Lord, my servant is lying home paralyzed dreadfully tormented."
>
> And Jesus said to him, "I will come and heal him."
>
> The centurion answered and said, "Lord, I am not worthy that you should come under my roof, but only speak a word, and my servant will

> be healed. For I am also a man under authority and having soldiers under me, and I say to this one, go, and he goes, and to another, come, and he comes, and to my servant, do this, and he does it."
>
> When Jesus heard it, he marveled and said to those who followed, "Assuredly, I say to you, I have not found such great faith, not even in Israel." (Matthew 8:5–10)

Why? Because the centurion recognized there was authority in the kingdom of God and he knew Jesus's authority was greater than his. He recognized that there are people under people and people over them, whom God has placed.

> And I say to you that many will come from East and West and sit down with Abraham, Isaac, and Jacob in the Kingdom of Heaven, but the sons of the kingdom will be cast into outer darkness. There will be weeping and gnashing of teeth. (Matthew 8:11–12)
>
> He chooses whom He chooses, but remember that He chooses, the least, to shame the wise; the weak, to shame the strong. (1 Corinthians 1:27)

As Paul said:

> For Christ did not send me to baptize, but to preach the gospel, not with the wisdom of words, lest the cross of Christ should be of no effect. My speech and my preaching were not with the persuasive words of human wisdom [soul power] but of demonstration of the spirit and power, that your faith should not rest in the wisdom of men, but in the power of God. Now we have

> received, not the spirit of the world, but the spirit who is from God that we might know the things that had been freely given to us by God. (1 Corinthians 1:17, 2:4–5, 2:12)
>
> This only I want to learn from you—did you receive the Holy Spirit by works of law or hearing of faith? Are you so foolish, having begun in the spirit, are you now being made perfect by the flesh? Have you suffered so many things in vain, if, indeed, it was in vain? Therefore, He who supplies the spirit to you and works miracles among you, does He do it by the works of the law or by the hearing of faith?—just as Abraham "believed God, and it was accounted to him for righteousness." (Galatians 3:2–6)

Beware of the tree of the knowledge of good and evil. Christianity isn't a matter of self-improvement but replacement. Don't try to improve what God has placed on the cross and crucified. Simply live by the life that's in you, the life of Jesus Christ, the tree of life.

Acknowledgment of God is one's whole lifestyle, not just being told that if he raises his hand, he is saved. One of the greatest deceptions Satan has put on the church of Jesus Christ is to make many people think they are saved. Men have used soul tactics like every head bowed, every eye closed. Now just slip that hand up. Make eye contact with me.

That steals God's glory, because people take their eyes off Jesus and put them on the person's preaching. That's why those people were saved. Remember, no man can save anyone; only Jesus Christ can save. In Revelations 18, there are merchants, and they sell men's souls. That's false salvation. Turn away from the soul realm and live in the spiritual realm.

Many have called themselves to the ministry, appearing as ministers of righteousness. That is rebellion in God's house. How do we recognize them?

First, they are self-seeking, always wanting preeminence. They aren't interested in the flock, just in building their ministry. They want money, recognition and to control the church of God for their benefit. There's a world of difference between God-anointed and self-appointed.

The following explains about those self-sent ones:

> For such are false apostles, deceitful workers, transforming themselves into apostles of Christ. And no wonder! For Satan himself transforms himself into an angel of light. Therefore, it is no great thing if his ministers also transform themselves into ministers of righteousness whose end will be according to their works. (2 Corinthians 11:13–15)

Many are deceived by what men say. What's important to God is what men are.

In Matthew 16:5–12, Jesus warned us to beware of the teachings of some religious leaders.

> Hypocrites [actors]! Well did Isaiah prophesy about you, saying: these people draw near to me with their mouth and honor me with their lips, but their heart is far from me.
>
> And in vain they worship Me, teaching as doctrines the commandments of men. (Matthew 15:7–9)
>
> And He said to them, "You are those who justify yourselves before men, but God knows your hearts, for what is highly esteemed among men [lusting after position and money] is an abomination in the sight of God." (Luke 16:15)

We don't need more celebrity preachers and performers. We need humble servants of the Lord who preach for God's glory, not their own.

Chapter Thirty-Two
Christ or Christianity?

It's very simple—Christ is in the Bible, and Christian is in the Bible, but Christianity is not. Christianity is what men have taken from Christ, from Christians, and from the Bible and formed into an organized religious system they can control and make money from. When the church was young, it was alive. It had no building, no New Testament, no hireling leaders or organizations.

Now, because of the traditions of men, the church seems old. Soon, those traditions will be gone, and once again, the church will be young, fresh, alive, and ready for her groom, the lion from the tribe of Judah, the Lord Jesus Christ.

"Your words were found, and I ate them, and your word was to me the joy and rejoicing of my heart; for I am called by your name, Oh Lord God of Hosts. I did not sit in the assembly of the mockers, nor did I rejoice; I sat alone because of Your hand, for You have filled me with indignation" (Jeremiah 15:16–17).

Chapter Thirty-Three
A Prophetic Message

God will judge the adulterous woman who appears to be His church. She left her first love to commit spiritual fornication with the world. God will strike her with affliction and sorrow. She claims to love Him, but she really loves herself. She's filled with self-interest and self-seeking. She brought the Babylonian garment and the wedge of gold into God's house. She loves the world, its riches and honor. God will strike many times.

The Lord's life was like that of a beautiful rose whose petals were burned to ashes for the purification of mankind. He died that we may live. Amen.

Chapter Thirty-Four
The Path

I feel as if my human nature is being crushed like grapes in the Lord's winepress. I feel my trials are like grains of wheat in His gristmill. It seems like the natural is ebbing away while the spiritual grows like the lily.

I hunger for the food of God's will, and I thirst for the drink of His holiness. I had a beginning, but because of His love, I will have no end.

I have found the path to the eternal will of God to be simple and pure. It is this: we receive perfection only through Jesus Christ.

The mystery to self-denial and mortification of my passions is granted through perseverance in Him.

His hands were fully extended on the cross for you.

Please reach back to Him.

When I was born, God gave me the name of Rene, which means "reborn" or "born again."

Rene of God.

Chapter Thirty-Five
An Open Letter—America

Dear Jack,

Many thanks for your ministry of exhortation. You always have an uplifting word, it word, it would seem.

What I am about to share with you is what the Lord has brought to me recently. Some of it is frightening, but we are not to worry, merely trust Him to see us through it, as He wills.

To begin with, we all have a desire to be accepted and loved. In these last days, we must all leave behind the people-pleasing business and seek only God's will and to please Him sincerely.

The following is what the Lord has shown me:

America has lost its soul. America has built for itself the idol of sin that it worships. America has rejected God. Sin was allowed to flourish and will destroy it from within. Racial unrest will erupt—ethnic group against ethnic group, race against race. Because of permissiveness, the rebellion will grow strong, and when it has grown powerful and reached its most vicious stage, God Himself will stop it. Many who appear to be Christian will show themselves barbaric. Men will appear as beasts of the field. All that religious man has built up by using God's name, but apart from His will, will come to nothing. God will allow this as He separates wheat from tares.

I was troubled by this and asked Jesus what I should do. His reply recently to me was this: "Tell my people to change their course, for the direction they are heading is sinful and wicked. They are not broken before Me and are filled with pride. Many seek Me simply because they are curious about Me, not out of love. I will gather the remnant for My special purpose. Faintness will come upon the world, but My children will find strength and rest in the ark of my salvation."

Brother Jack, in this world, you know I have little strength and am of low position. These few words of exhortation are for the body of Christ for preparation, as the Father loves them so and wishes to prepare them.

Be assured of our prayers for both you and Ann. Press on to the finish.

Love,
Rene Bates

Chapter Thirty-Six
Quiet Years

Embrace the divine breeze of eternity, and He will fill the emptiness of your life with the quiet years of His own. As we quiet our lives into His stillness, only then do we realize that we are not listening, knowing not that He was continually speaking. Our Lord desires us to have an ear to hear what the Spirit is saying. The way into His divine presence is through the doorway of obscurity and the pathway of insignificance. Love the will of God, and He will guard your heart from the sinking passions of your own plans and will.

If you would see Jesus, your heart must be filled with love for Him, your mouth speaking words of gold, frankincense, and mirth. Do you not know that waiting on the Lord strengthens the heart and brings it into submission and obedience? The meaning of love is relationship with Jesus and His transforming devotion. The amount of peace to be received is in proportion to the amount of surrender that is offered to Him. Withdraw the soul from empty pleasures and allow it to rest in His holy presence. A discontented, complaining person brings about a lonesome manner of living, but the life of a Christian is filled with hope while exhorting all to holiness. To have the mind of Christ, one must spend quiet years waiting before Him and willing to be used, or not be used, as He desires. To speak many words or to be quiet, to laugh or to weep, to be esteemed or to be ridiculed, to suffer for a time or to have perfect health—in all these circumstances, God speaks from His divine mind to those who have an ear to hear. We do not hear from God simply because we are so very occupied with ourselves, what we want, and our efforts at attaining them. Why not spend quiet years waiting upon God and fully dependent upon Him? Desire His presence in the soul. Let nothing come between the soul and Him, between innocence and inspiration. Willingly yield to the cross of trials and afflictions of this life, knowing all comes from His hand. As the soul rests in the heart of God, it learns never to return into captivity.

In general, temptations, weakness, and faults are never overcome by willpower or efforts but by quietly turning to God and His power. When the believer learns to trust the Sovereign Master, His strength quickly flows into the believer's soul, and evil is taken away. Order, love, and wisdom soon follow, knowing all good things come from above. The soul then is able to bear all things and begins to understand that patience is trusting God for all that happens. The quiet years are filled with inexhaustible water of the Lord's own goodness and refreshment.

Silently listen to the quiet voice of God, and tongues of men who speak of religious things will be much less important. To do something religious for God is easy to do, but to give up our own will, yes, this is very hard to do. Let the soul soar in its journey to knowing God, and do not be disheartened or despair of your present condition. We all have weaknesses that have surprised us and feelings that there are those sins that we do not see as yet. The soul that waits upon the Lord in quietness will never experience disappointment but will enjoy the expectation of blessings. And as God speaks to the soul, He will give truth and some fresh insight, thereby cleansing the soul by His light and making for a more joyful service to Him.

Allow the soul to response in Him, being very tranquil and marked by little activity, trying not to be showy but modest. Then, He will take your will, give you His, and restore you to fullness. This is peace in the quiet years.

Let the soul fellowship with the spirit, and He will always lead to Jesus and the Father. God has already given whatever we need to live a godly life. Then what is it we lack? The will to do so. We offer up our sins to Him, but our will—oh, that is something so very difficult. Permit the soul a period of self-examination, no matter how distasteful it is. The Lord Jesus knows us, but it is we who do not know ourselves. How do we exchange our will for His? Crucifixion of the self. Quiet years are granted through a life of grace, and that life is His. The Shepherd has the right to choose which pasture to place His sheep, but we are blinded by our own will. You see, it is not our will that brings perfect peace but obedience to His.

The spirit of prayer passes through the heart of Jesus to forever commune with God's infinite love and wisdom. Talk with Him. He is waiting.

The Flames of God's Fire

Who makes … His ministers aflame of fire.
—Psalm 104:4

Preface
A Symphony of Love and Truth

Even though the eyes of men are closed, the light of God shines on humanity just as the stars shine in the darkness to enlighten the night. It's dark outside, but the internal darkness of unregenerate man produces a desert within, a dryness of faith, and a continual thirst. The mantle of night covers the earth with deep darkness, producing dismal prayers, vain imaginings, and the clouded fog of misery. May the dawn bring the golden glory of a new day.

The sages of our age suffer the loneliness of exile, and the seers are bruised into quietness, wounded like sparrows that have fallen to the ground. The petition of our hearts is to unlock the gates of heaven—if they are closed—with the tears of contrition, from the mystery of sleep men call life.

I am heartsick for my Lord and homesick for heaven. The frailty of the human heart is crushed beyond earthly encouragement because of man's vanity.

Whether it is day or night, let us put away the disguises of pride and self-seeking and receive the way of truth and the grace of life in meekness, wrapping our hearts in Jesus's compassion.

Drop by drop, let the dew of heaven merge into the river of life, quieting our restlessness, saying "Peace. Be still" to the fires of our lust. Winds will come to fan the flames of God's love, exhaling the flesh and inhaling His Spirit, teaching us that correct power reveals itself in meekness, that genuine wisdom reveals itself in godly simplicity and, finally, that accurate valor shows itself by gentleness.

Merciful Jesus, deliver us from those who desire leadership, and then unite us as Your followers as we sojourn through life, enlightened by Your wisdom and gracious consolation. "We are fools for Christ's sake, but you are wise in Christ. We are weak, but you are strong. You are distinguished, but we are dishonored. Even to the present hour, we hunger and thirst, and we are poorly clothed, and beaten, and homeless. And we labor, working with our own hands" (1 Corinthians 4:10–12).

Chapter Thirty-Seven
Learning

Many have been taught to search for God outwardly, but God is within every believer. Whoever is joined to the Lord Jesus Christ is one spirit with Him. Your spirit and His Holy Spirit are joined and are always in communication. So long as men value self-interest, self-seeking and harbor selfish ambition in their hearts, then to that extent, they hinder God's progress in their lives. They say "Glory to God" or "God will be glorified if we do this." Usually, they mean that they desire the glory for themselves. Are we willing to be nothing in God's eyes? Let me press a little deeper. Are we willing to be nothing before people?

In time, the spirit realm should become natural to the believer. That occurs naturally when a Christian learns to attain a position lower than humility, when he learns to be dead to his desires and to himself. He must learn that the life of Jesus is his life. If we suffer, we must learn that God is teaching us obedience, because He wants us perfect. We should rest in His arms and move only when He moves, then everything will be the same to us, whether we are rich or poor, in health or sickness, in our homes or in a faraway land. Then God has become our life.

It's impossible for a Christian to look up at God when the same person looks down on people.

Dear Jesus, may Your words to us now be as apples of gold, producing within us oaks of righteousness and passion for You.

Chapter Thirty-Eight
Scholastic Knowledge

Knowledge is good. Only when people boast and are prideful of it does it become, for them, a stumbling block.

In that hour, Jesus rejoiced in the Spirit and said, "I praise you, Father, Lord of heaven and earth, that you have hidden these things from the wise and prudent and revealed them to babes. Even so, Father, for it seemed good in Your sight" (Luke 10:21).

Why are the deeper spiritual truths hidden from some men of great theological learning? Because they've become proud of their accomplishments. They give information, droning on during their speeches, entertaining crowds. That seems to correlate with the Bible, but the people remain empty. It is man's interpretation of what God said, not what He said. Such men seek position, recognition, and reputation because they preach for their own glory. Please, Jesus, give us preachers who will preach for Your glory.

There are men who always seek information about God, yet they never become godly. They are lukewarm and prideful. Jesus was meek and gentle, and where He is, there is liberty and gentleness. The supernatural becomes quite natural.

I have found that many seek the gifts of the Holy Spirit for their own glory. They seek Jesus for what they can get from Him. Sometimes, I cry. Who is your greatest enemy? It is yourself. To be a Christian, we must take up our own crosses and follow Him. We must die to ourselves. No one should try to improve what God placed on the cross and crucified. We must replace our lives with His and crucify our love of self.

The final harvest is near, when Shiloh gathers His heritage, ripe with the seasons of God's grace and matured by the rains of His fruitfulness.

Chapter Thirty-Nine
Crucified and Crossed Out

> Be of the same mind toward one another. Do not set your mind on high things, but associate with the humble. Do not be wise in your own opinion.
> —Romans 12:16

We have a natural tendency to look up to our superiors. We bestow honor, recognition, and titles on them. What do we do for those whom we think are our inferiors? We try to teach them instead of learn from them.

Who is being wise? It's fearful to look down on someone in whom God dwells. We must be crossed out by the cross, and everything we idolize must go there—our ability, wisdom, knowledge, works, and belief in how good we are.

Only God is good. We must be God-centered, not self-centered. Do not examine yourself by the tree of knowledge of good and evil; examine yourself by the wood of the cross. When you look at the cross, do you see Jesus? If so, good.

Do you also see yourself? Do we really understand what took place there? I think not. Have people ever wondered why men curse the name of Jesus Christ and never mention His most holy blood? Demons make people curse His name, but they are terrified of His blood. They were conquered by it, because it is alive.

The blood of Christ provided reconciliation, redemption, justification, sanctification, victory, eternal life, and communion with God, the Father. His blood is also innocent, precious, and final for the forgiveness of our sins. At the Lord's Supper, we drink the cup of the new covenant in His blood and remember and proclaim His death until He returns.

Our aim, all too often, is to be holy, spiritual or to have victory over some fault or weakness. God has one aim—to pour the life of Jesus into those He has chosen and who have chosen Him.

Those who are poor in spirit are blessed. The Lord has purged them of all man-made doctrines, and they can see the Lord in a new way.

One of the first things they see is that church leadership isn't perpetual but spiritual. It should change with the spirits leading, as it did under Peter, James, Paul, and John. There is a price for that—rejection and persecution from man's traditions. If Christ wills, one suffers outside the gate and bears His reproach. If he does so, then one day, he'll share in His glory. Although we are only human, we have God's life and His nature in us.

Who was the first person to have Jesus living inside them? It was Mary, His mother. God's intention is to have Himself inside every believer so that He may become our life. He is inside our spirit, wanting to become our life, but so much of modern preaching is conversion without conviction, forgiveness without repentance, and renewal without restitution.

Chapter Forty
The Temple

Recently, as I waited on the Lord, I was given visions of heaven. I walked and saw colors I never saw before. It looked like I was on a garden path.

As I looked to my left, I saw Jesus walking beside me, holding my left hand in His right. I looked down and saw His robe, which was pure white with gold edging and golden threads woven throughout, and His feet.

I never looked at His face. He spoke to me as we walked, "Tell My people if they want to honor Me, they must stop going their own ways. They must cease seeking their own pleasure and refrain from speaking their own words."

I looked off into the distance to the right and saw a clear, amber-like huge city. Jesus lifted His left hand and pointed to the left. "Behold."

When I looked, I saw a blue-gray mist. It lifted, and I saw the bottom of God's throne. On the foundation were written the words *righteousness* and *justice*. It was one thousand times larger than any chair I had ever seen. I saw two huge feet, but when I looked higher, everything was covered by the mist.

As suddenly as it came, the vision ended. I pondered it for days without telling my wife, Pauline, or anyone else.

On the third night after the vision, the Lord spoke to my heart, "Read Ezekiel 43."

I did so and came to verses 5–7. As I read them, my heart pounded.

The spirit lifted me up and brought me into the inner court, and behold, the glory of the Lord filled the temple.

Then I heard Him speaking to me from the temple while a man stood beside me.

And He said to me, "Son of Man, this is the place of my throne and the place of the soles of my feet, where I will dwell in the midst of the children of Israel forever. No more shall the house of Israel defile My holy name, nor their kings by their harlotry or with the carcasses of their kings on their high place."

I exhort the elders and Christians. It is time to remove the idols of self that are hidden deep within the heart. There are greater abominations that dwell there—pride, adultery, selfish ambitions, envies, and contentions.

I know that message will upset some, but I am merely the messenger, and I must deliver it as it was given to me. I tell you, because I love you.

Chapter Forty-One
Is There Anything Good in Us?

Our journey through this life mustn't be through one particular teaching or the doctrine of one sect or movement. Our walk through life must be by God's Holy Spirit, then we must live by that Spirit.

We must first realize that we, in ourselves, can't produce love, joy, peace, long-suffering, kindness, goodness, faithfulness, gentleness, or self-control. Those are the fruits of the Spirit (Galatians 4:22–23), not our fruit. As we learn to walk and live by the Spirit, we become one with our Lord and pleasing to Him. He enjoys seeing His life in us.

We must remember that God desires more than we do and that we should walk holy before Him. One shouldn't try to walk alone—we can't do anything by ourselves. If we can't do anything to remove our sins, what makes people think they can do anything good in thought, word, or deed apart from the Holy Spirit? One can teach a dog to walk on its hind legs like a man, but sooner or later, the dog will go down to all fours. It is a dog, not a man.

We do the same when we try to live like a Christian by our own efforts. In the end, we fail. However, we can let Jesus live through us. We must remember that nothing good dwells in us (Romans 7:18).

Let us serve God in the newness of Spirit, not the oldness of the letter (Romans 7:6). In Greek, the word *letter* means "epistle," "learning," or "scripture." That phrase means we mustn't be proud of great learning, even of scripture, because we then look down on others.

Catholics won't go to heaven, nor will Protestants or Pentecostals. Christians go to heaven.

Thank you, Jesus.

Chapter Forty-Two
Reflections

To realize there is nothing good in us takes a long time and learning from bitter experience. God knows us, but we don't know ourselves. If the Lord manifested Himself in a real way, I know His holiness and beauty would convince us of our frailties. One's efforts at goodness will delay God's working in one's life. We must cease from our works, be still, and know that Jesus is Lord.

When a master artist wants to paint a masterpiece, his first step is to make the canvas still. If the canvas said, "I'll help the artist by moving and being busy. I want to hurry him along and work for him."

When the artist finds the canvas isn't secure, he makes it tighter. The canvas is worthless until the master begins to work on it, and the canvas must learn to be still.

Sometimes, the Master Artist uses sharp tools on His canvas of Christians, but in His heart, He knows what He wants to paint. Some of His colors are white, black, yellow, and red, representing the races of mankind. They don't realize the masterpiece He is making to show them to all in the universe.

In the end, there is only one painting, and the time has come for the Artist to frame it. That frame is solid gold, set with precious stones representing Jesus, who protects and hugs the painting.

The Artist then takes the once-worthless, empty canvas to a mirror and lets the painting see how beautiful it is. There are many reflections to be seen within. The painting can't believe what it saw—the Master Artist painted Himself.

God did it all—man's salvation, sanctification, and completion. God requires nothing of man except to allow Him to work His masterpiece into people. We shouldn't try to help Him. All He needs is one thing—the cross where the canvas must be nailed.

The more one struggles, the worse it will hurt. We should be still and know He is in control. We should trust Him, because He is the spirit of truth and will lead us into all truth (John 16:13). We must believe He will do all good things for us.

When we sin, we have removed ourselves from the cross. We must become dead to sin. Can sin tempt a dead man? Through Jesus Christ, we are alive to God.

Lastly, but most importantly, we must remember that faith is but a reflection of God's grace.

Chapter Forty-Three
We Are Free

The book of Galatians teaches that we are dead to the religious world through the cross of Christ. As our hearts open to Him, we reflect back His love and peace. We become one with Christ through faith in Him.

Those who choose to love serving God rather than God, who choose to love their denomination or sect more than God will eventually love themselves more than God.

Without God, there are two things we must know—inside, we are evil; outside, we are deceitful. With God living His life through us, all times are the same. When we work, we pray through our spirits. We cast ourselves totally to Him, believing He won't deceive or hurt us.

Oh, precious Jesus, You who suffered so much for us, forgive us, dear Jesus, for our sins that broke Your heart. Let us find consolation in Your cross, which You bore for us. Give us strength to bear our hurts for Your glory. Teach us, precious Jesus, that everything that is good comes from Your hands. You are the medicine that heals our wounds.

Beautiful Jesus, teach us to be content wherever we are, knowing You put us there. Give us hearts filled with love for You, that we worship You in truth, not just with words. Teach us, dear Lord, of Your love, which is so deep that it first appears to be cold. In reality, it is so calm that its holy fire purges all sin from us.

Grant us, through Your graces and mercies, unbroken communion with You, and teach us to love. Amen.

Chapter Forty-Four
Persecution

The leaders of the early church never prepared a speech using their natural abilities and human knowledge. They had no prepared organizations. What they did was give a place to the Holy Spirit to speak what God wanted at that time.

That can only happen when there is freedom in a meeting. Men must give up control of the meeting and allow God to do what He wills. The elders must only teach as those who learn. They are examples to the flock in judging what is said at the meeting. Above all, they shouldn't dominate or control the meeting.

How is the Holy Spirit grieved? He is told, "Holy Spirit, You are welcome here." After that, He is quenched by those in control, because they ignore Him and won't release control to Him.

If I invited you to my home and said "You're welcome here," you'd be happy to come inside. Then, after you were inside, if I dominated the conversation and wouldn't let you say anything, you would feel quenched. If I ignored you, you'd feel grieved.

A day of persecution is coming to all true believers in Christ, and the persecution will come from false Christians, the deceivers who deceive themselves and others. They will persecute true believers in Jesus Christ, and they'll do it in His name.

In John 15:21, Jesus said, "But all these things they will do to you for My name's sake, because they do not know Him who sent Me."

Jesus also mentions those people in Mark 7:6–7, "This people honors Me with their lips, but their heart is far from Me, and in vain they worship Me."

They will persecute us and think they are doing God's work. That is the way it has been throughout history. Their fire is false—they merely pretend to be Christian. Jesus calls them hypocrites or actors. Those who are truly called by God will know the pretenders, and that seems to bring hostility upon them.

"Then you shall again discern between the righteous and the wicked, between one who serves God, and one who does not serve Him" (Malachi 3:18).

In the last years, I have had to withdraw from certain friends because when I was near them, I felt grieved in spirit. They were selfish and filled with self-love. I sensed they came to Jesus only for what they could get out of Him. A few times, I tried to show them a better way, but because of their feelings of superiority, I couldn't get through to them. It was as if God was leading me away just in time.

I felt sad for them. Perhaps I will try again.

Chapter Forty-Five

God's Breaking

I know a man who lives in the desert. He is there because that's the place where God wants him. He's there not only for his sake but for the sake of other Christians who live in the city. He is there that he might hear from God without man intruding into his spirit. His life and only hope is God. He isn't involved in religious activities, but he offers up his life to waiting, listening, and praying. He has abandoned his life and attached himself to the Lord.

Occasionally, he leaves the desert, goes to the city, and stays with a church organization for a while. During his stays, the leaders seem to know he's different, but they didn't know what to do with him. He told them his thoughts, and at first, they agreed. God's power—through signs, wonders, and miracles—validated his ministry, but that made them envious.

Finally, he left again for their sake, fearing they would rebel against what God wanted. Afterward, they found some scripture to justify their action or inaction. Justification is always easy.

He went back to the desert to wait, listen, and pray to God.

Jesus took seven loaves of bread and broke them to feed the multitude. There are also men who must be broken enough to feed the flock and to sound the alarm to many who are sleeping with the concubines of reputation, security, and recognition. They have a licentious liaison with condescending concupiscence, dancing to marionette chains of their own making.

Chapter Forty-Six
Love

Those who try to know Jesus by intellectual effort find, after a long time, that knowledge isn't enough. One must come to Jesus empty of self so that he may fill the vessel with Himself. If the seeker values his reputation, his pride prevents him from seeing the Divine One.

If a person wants to be with the one he seeks, he must only love Him. To know Him, a Christian must love Him. To know about Him, he only needs to read with his mind. A Christian must read with a heart filled with love, not for knowledge, so that he may quote chapter and verse to impress others. Love is the better way to understanding.

There is praying with the mind, but praying by the Spirit requires love.

There is a kind of preaching from the mind, but in the end, the preacher seeks to steal God's glory. Preaching by the Spirit requires love.

Out of a Christian's innermost being shall flow rivers of living water to break the earthen dam of men's traditions.

So, there was a division among the people because of Him (John 7:43).

The Bible teachers of Jesus's day became prideful from their knowledge of scripture.

They answered and said to him, "Are you also from Galilee? Search and look, for no prophet has arisen out of Galilee" (John 7:42).

They were wrong—a great prophet came from Galilee. His name was Jonah (2 Kings 14:25).

All too often, the same things happen today. Scriptures are bent to profit those who would benefit by it. The law kills, but the Spirit gives life.

Jesus said to them, "If you were blind, you would have no sin; but now you say, 'We see!' Therefore, your sin remains" (John 9:41).

"They will put you out of the synagogues; yes, the time is coming that whoever kills you will think that he offers God service" (John 16:2).

Jesus said, "I pray for them. I do not pray for the world, but for those whom you have given me, for they were yours" (John 17:9).

Chapter Forty-Seven
Repentance

Believe in the Lord your God, and you shall be established; believe His prophets, and you shall prosper (2 Chronicles 20:20).

Surely the Lord God does nothing unless He reveals His secret to His servants the prophets (Amos 3:7).

There are many who desire the day of the Lord, but for them, that day will be darkness, not light. Many professing Christians—those who claim to be Christian but are not—shouldn't say God is their Father. God becomes our Father only when we are born again.

The Lord is coming soon, but before that coming, He calls for repentance now. He'll send fire upon the church to purify the leadership and purge them from sin that they may make their offerings to the Lord in righteousness.

To the extent they repent, they won't be judged, but God's judgment will surely come. There are three major areas of repentance for the church:

- Sorcery—The so-called church is filled with sorcerers, most not realizing what they are doing. Some possess supernatural power. There are only two kinds of supernatural power: God's or Satan's. The enemy infiltrates the body through the soul of man, through his thinking, wants, and ambitions. Lucifer rebelled against God by his self-will, not God's will. Five times, he said, "I will" (Isaiah 14:13–15). That is sorcery.

  Man's pride, his self-will and selfish ambition, makes man rebel against God repeatedly. Religious man has to repent and submit to God's will, not his own. Rebellion is as the sin of witchcraft, and arrogance like the evil of idolatry. (1 Samuel 15:23)

- Adultery—There is much adultery in the church, physical and spiritual. Many lust after one another in their hearts. God sees that and gives them time to repent. Spiritual adultery comes when some of those in the church love the world so much they become worldly, even in their assembly before God. Their meetings are glitzy social affairs, with Jesus thrown in to justify their clubs. Some are travel clubs, and some are social clubs, but they always exclude the needy.
- Perjury—These are perjurers and those who take oaths falsely. They promise God to do something or not to do something else. They include the self-appointed in their leadership, those who say, "God called me to the ministry."

  If He hasn't called them, they have just perjured themselves before Him, and their ministry is false. Remember Lucifer's "I will" statement? Fallen man loves to exalt himself and be like God, having people watch while he performs, stealing God's words, worship, and glory. If they would simply fear God, their fear would help them repent.

  Today, we call the proud blessed, and those who are in rebellion are raised up and rewarded by giving them recognition, titles, and money.

  As we approach the end, God will grant the gift of discernment to more and more believers. They shall discern between the wicked and the righteous, between those who serve Jesus as Lord and those who use God for their own ends.

  Are they proud of their reputations because they give them positions of honor? Jesus made no reputation for Himself. He alone is our example (Phil. 2:7).

Chapter Forty-Eight
The World

The reason so many are out of God's order in the church is because they have done what is good, not what is right. God has a plan for all His children, but we often choose what is good for us at the expense of what is right. Choosing good often brings us the good life. Choosing right often brings death to our will and life to our spirit. We aren't supposed to eat of the tree of knowledge of good and evil. The good we do, at the expense of the right God would have us do, brings evil.

Eating from the tree of life—His body and blood—brings abundant life. As we enter into the four winds of heaven at the center of God's breath, His life becomes ours. His heart becomes ours, and His will, ours too.

The only thing that can rob or deceive us from entering into His life is the world. The word *world* in 1 John 2:15–17 means "orderly arrangement or system." It's taken from the Greek word *kosmos*. We should read that passage with that in mind.

> Do not love the world or the things in the world. If anyone loves the world, the love of the Father is not in him.
>
> For all that is in the world—the lust of the flesh, the lust of the eyes, and the pride of life—is not of the Father, but is of the world.
>
> And the world is passing away, and the lust of it; but he who does the will of God abides forever. (1 John 2:15–17)

Organized religion deceives Christians into thinking they must join a man-made, man-glorified organization. In verse 26, John warns about "those who try to deceive you." In verse 27, he writes, "The Holy Spirit is our teacher, and not man." Men love to have the preeminence. Yes, even today, we have many Diotrephes (3 John 9–10).

We are living under the new covenant, new testament, and God has spoken.

> None of them shall teach his neighbor, and none his brother, saying "Know the Lord," for all shall know Me, from the least of them to the greatest of them. (Hebrews 8:11)

What of the hirelings? Perhaps we don't need so many.

We should keep in mind the meaning of *world* as an orderly arrangement or system when we read John 15:18.

> If the world hates you, you know that it hated Me before it hated you.

That passage refers to the religious leaders whom Jesus exposed and who had Him crucified.

> If you were of the world, the world would love its own. Yet because you are not of the world, but I chose you out of the world, therefore the world hates you. (John 15:19)

That refers to Jesus choosing us out of organized religions, with their systems of what to do and when, filling our heads with knowledge from the tree of good and evil. The only life God accepts is the life of Christ, the tree of life.

> Remember the word that I said to you. "A servant is not greater than his master." If they persecuted

> Me, they will also persecute you. If they kept My word, they will keep yours also. (John 15:20)
>
> Those with positions and titles persecuted Jesus, as did those who made money from the system. People were going to Jesus, and the leaders feared losing their positions. (John 11:48)
>
> But all these things they will do to you for My name's sake, because they do not know Him who sent Me. (John 15:21)

Jesus prophesied that apostate Christian leaders would be the ones who would persecute others—doing it in His name. The self-righteous ones will quote scriptures as they do so, just as they did to Him. The ones who do so aren't saved, because they don't know the Father who sent Jesus.

> If I had not come and spoken to them, they would have no sin, but now they have no excuse for their sin. (John 15:22)

They have God's Word to read, but they don't have the heart to understand.

> He who hates Me hates my Father also.
>
> If I had not done among them the works which no one else did, they would have no sin; but now they have seen and also hated both Me and My Father.
>
> But this has happened that the word might be fulfilled which is written in their law, "They hated Me without cause." (John 15:23–25)
>
> They will put you out of the synagogues. The time is coming when whoever kills you will think he offers God service. (John 16:2)

They cannot digest you, make you as one of them. In the end, Jesus will vomit them out of His mouth, because they will not lose themselves in Him. (Revelations 3:16)

Chapter Forty-Nine
The Showmen

Only those who have an ear to hear what the Spirit is saying to the churches will be able to understand the next part (Revelations 2:7).

In Revelations 2:2, Jesus commends those who "test those who say they are apostles and are not and have found them liars." Then He goes on (Revelations 2:6) and says, "But this you have, that you hate the deeds of the Nicolaitans, which I also hate."

Apostle means "messenger," "one who is sent." How often has a hireling pastor said that he is only the messenger of what is being said or that "God called [him] to the ministry"? We are exhorted by Jesus to test them to see if they are really God-anointed or self-appointed.

If the church doesn't test those who say God sent them, then the church will be divided into clergy and laity, one lording over the other. *Nicolaitans* means "victory over the people." Jesus said he hated that and we should too. If the deeds of the Nicolaitans aren't stopped (Revelations 2:6), they will eventually become doctrines of the Nicolaitans (Revelations 2:15), which means they will officially teach the church division of clergy versus laity. Once again, Jesus says he hates that (Revelations 2:15).

This is a truth. Most pastors are welded to the doctrines they have learned and are fossilized within the theology of their particular assembly.

Chapter Fifty
Who Are the Hirelings?

The thief does not come except to steal and to kill and to destroy. I have come that they may have life and that they may have *it* more abundantly.

> I am the good shepherd. The good shepherd gives His life for the sheep. But a hireling, *he who is* not the shepherd, one who does not own the sheep, sees the wolf coming and leaves the sheep and flees; and the wolf catches the sheep and scatters them. The hireling flees because he is a hireling and does not care about the sheep. (John 10:10–13, emphasis added)

The thief who comes to kill, steal, and destroy is the hireling; the wolf is the devil. Hireling is one who is paid wages. Check concordance.

Hirelings are those whose primary interest is money. There are servants who love the Lord, and for them, my heart is happy. Those who claim to be Christians but aren't are thieves and robbers. Those who have received Jesus Christ as Lord have everlasting life.

We must listen to His voice and hear His word. Our words must also, in time, be spirit and give life to those who hear us. Most words are of the flesh and profit nothing of eternal value. We must be diligent to flee from the voices of strangers and thieves who come to steal, kill, and destroy (John 10:10).

He steals from God's Word to exalt himself; he kills, by his words and doctrines, the freedom in the life of Christ. He destroys truth that will set people free by his doctrines emanating from the tree of the knowledge of good and evil, bringing death, not life.

That tree represents Satan, the author of death. The tree of life represents Jesus, the author of life. Four thousand years later, God was on earth as a man. Again, He said, "Eat, this is my body" (Matthew 26:26). Most refused, thinking worldly.

The hireling isn't the true shepherd or pastor, because he doesn't own the sheep. Wolves come and catch some, causing division in others. The hireling shepherd only wants to build his own ministry, wanting more sheep to feed his ego and gain fame.

Our Lord made Himself of no reputation (Phil. 2:7). Those who belong to God hear His voice, and that voice whispers, "There is only one flock and only one true Shepherd."

Bible teachers, or Pharisees, said, "This man is not from God, because He doesn't keep the Sabbath" (John 9:16). They ate from the tree of knowledge of good and evil, not life.

Some of my writings have been likened to a steel fist within a velvet glove. If that's so, it is only directed toward hypocrisy within religion and man's many traditions.

Chapter Fifty-One
Attaining to Positions

> And you, Capernaum, who are exalted to heaven, will be thrust down to hades.
>
> —Luke 10:15

There are two ways to obtain a position of prominence within the church. One is by works and self-effort; the other is by God's calling and anointing. The prideful of heart are always jealous of God's anointed and seek ways to discredit and hinder them.

When God calls a person, He anoints and empowers him to fulfill His desires. Those who have worked for their positions will feel threatened by the person God wants, knowing, in their hearts, that they only attained their positions by their own efforts. They will use intimidation and anything else to keep their positions too.

The one who is called by God has his position given by God without such effort. He would probably attain that position in the end, even though it would probably come at the time of judgment. Then, God will expose by fire the motivations of everyone's heart. Then there will be no more self-deceptions.

Here is a spiritual law: Those who have worked for position, using self-effort, will always feel threatened by the one who receives his position from God's choice. Somehow, both know it inwardly. The self-appointed will feel the God-anointed wants his job, but nothing could be further from the truth. The God-anointed just wants to fulfill his calling. Instead, he finds envy and jealousy from the self-appointed, hindering God's greater work for His kingdom.

King Saul hated David without reason. He was envious of David, knowing he was anointed by God. David never did anything to take away Saul's kingdom, but David knew, in his heart, that the kingdom was already his.

Saul seemed to know that too. His pride made him want to have it all. He wasn't content just to be king; he wanted to also offer sacrifices to God, the job of the prophets. Saul wanted all the attention.

Today, it seems like the sons of Saul hate the sons of David and do the same things.

The Pharisees, the religious leaders, were the sons of Saul and hated—without cause—the Son of David, Jesus Christ. Kings in their little kingdoms always resist God's anointed. Man's ambition rebels against God's will, but He always gives man freedom of choice until the end.

"Beware of false prophets who come to you in sheep's clothing, but inwardly they are ravenous wolves" (Matthew 7:15).

"He who hears you hears Me, he who rejects you rejects Me, and he who rejects Me rejects Him who sent Me" (Luke 10:16).

Jesus warned us to beware of certain Bible teachers after we have come to Him. Once we go to Jesus, Lucifer will try to lead the believer into error by false teaching.

"Then they understood that He did not tell them to beware of the leaven of bread, but of the doctrine of the Pharisees and Sadducees" (Matthew 16:12).

"False teachers will always say their teachings are the truth of God's word, but His judgment will eventually be on them" (Ezekiel 11:1–13).

They like to separate themselves from the people and hide behind the wall of religion. How should we recognize them?

They love organizations, buildings, and things. They would rather use people than use things and love people. Another way to know them is that they aren't willing to step down from leadership. They become dictatorial, refusing to allow other ministries to prosper. Everything in church meetings becomes predictable. As a result, those meetings turn into a repeating liturgical melody of sameness.

Chapter Fifty-Two
Spirit of Divination

It is possible for someone to claim that the holy scriptures are inspired by God and that he is a follower of Paul. He can say there is only one way to be saved and look very much like a Christian yet still be a sorcerer who possesses the power of divination.

One way to recognize such people is how they use God, His Word and gifts, for profit. That statement will offend some people, but they should read the following:

> Now it happened, as we went to prayer, that a certain slave girl possessed with a spirit of divination met us, who brought her masters much profit by fortune-telling.
>
> This girl followed Paul and us, and cried out, saying, "These men are the servants of the most High God, who proclaim to us the way of salvation."
>
> And this she did for many days, but Paul, greatly annoyed, turned and said to the spirit, "I command you in the name of Jesus Christ to come out of her," and he came out that very hour.
>
> But when her masters saw their hope of profit was gone, they seized Paul and Silas and dragged them into the marketplace to the authorities. (Acts 16:16–19)

Most, although not all, churches have sorcerers in them unknown to the assembly. They tithe, flatter the leadership, and appear to be Christians. When Christians lift up their hands to worship the Lord, the deceivers worship Satan. When the Christians pray in tongues, the deceivers do also but pray to the devil.

That explains why there is no power in the church. While Christians are unaware of it, deceivers sow seeds of derision, lust, and confusion into the assembly. The church has no idea it's happening.

Why would the Holy Spirit offer the gift of discerning of spirits (1 Corinthians 12:10) if people can figure out things intellectually? All of God's gifts should be used as He wills, not as we think, so that there is balance in the body.

A few years ago, I was giving Bible study at a young couple's home. There were fifteen people at the class. A young man came in, sat quietly, and listened. Outwardly, he seemed Christian, but I felt uneasy looking at him. Something was wrong. Inwardly, I asked the Lord what to do. I got the feeling I should continue the class.

Two hours later, as the meeting was almost over, the young man said he wanted to say something. He told us he worshipped Satan and read satanic books. He said he wanted to demonstrate the power of darkness by stopping our Bible study that evening. After hearing the class, he said he was convinced God's power was stronger than darkness, and he asked if it was possible for him to become a Christian.

We prayed, and the young man received the Lord—we think. He never came back to our class, and we still pray for him.

You have wearied the Lord with your words, yet you say, "In what way have we wearied Him?" In that you say "Everyone who does evil is good in the sight of the Lord, and He delights in them" or "Where is the God of justice?" (Malachi 2:17).

As Christians, we must realize that the God within us is greater than the enemy, who is in the world.

"Surely, the Lord is coming quickly" (Revelations 22:20).

Healthy sheep follow the shepherd's voice, but weak or sick sheep will follow a stranger's voice. They are starved from not feeding on God and have no spiritual growth despite their increase in numbers. Although they seem alive, they are dead.

We must assemble in the name of the Lord, but not to build an organization or because it is traditional to do so. We should not be deceived by men's titles or their words. We should walk with God, not men's traditions. Jesus isn't like the descriptions learned theologians give Him.

What was He like? He ate with sinners, cast demons from people, allowed a sinful woman to wash His feet, healed on the Sabbath, ate with unwashed hands, and called the Bible teachers of his day liars, children of the devil, and hypocrites.

He is the same today. He left religionists and went to sinners. At least they weren't hypocritical and were willing to listen. Religionists handle God's Word deceitfully because they want their sheep to remain with them, stuck within the confines of their organization or tradition. Jesus said we would know the truth, and the truth—Jesus—would set us free.

Deep darkness fills the minds of many. Right becomes wrong, false appears true, and false prophets preach as ministers of righteousness. The world is brought into the church by traditional religionists. Men stand before others and boast about their faith then beg for money to build an empire.

That isn't faith. Sometimes, they say, "It's critical that you give. If you don't, some people might not get saved."

That is how they turn people into merchandise. No one should add a heavy load to someone else's back. We should help the poor as an example for others. Those who give in order to get are bound by greed.

Chapter Fifty-Three
Sons of Judas

Our relationship with God can never be determined by the organization to which we belong or the words we say, nor is it determined by our apparent dedication to studying, teaching, or preaching.

Judas looked like a Christian outwardly, someone who did the right thing, but inwardly, he was a traitor. Today, sons of Judas are within the church, wanting preeminence and using God for their benefit.

If people would only try to please God, not man, they would learn that we are perfect in Christ but imperfect before men.

Men love to boast of their supposed accomplishments with converts, healings, and gathering crowds of people. Such things only exalt the preacher. He speaks from within himself, and he is self-glorifying. The modern church system is full of preachers who seek God's gifts for their own benefit. They preach for gain and heal for fame. Most only pretend to have God's gifts—they hope God will do something to validate their ministry.

Occasionally, God honors someone's faith because He wants to heal him. Quickly, the preacher stands up and steals God's glory, even though he says, "Glory to God." By cunning and craftiness, just like Judas, they deceive even the elect, if possible.

Healing campaigns are nothing more than moneymaking efforts. Men entertain their assemblies while stealing inwardly God's glory. Satan, through his sons, is coming with power, signs, and lying wonders. How many preachers really want to benefit mankind and not promote their own ministry? We should praise God that there are at least a few.

Why do so many preachers focus on buildings and money? Why do they want titles before their names? Why do they exalt gifts and ministries? Why don't they offer prayer with Jesus to cause repentance then revival?

Jesus was a miracle worker and healer. He was also an apostle, prophet, evangelist, pastor, and teacher. He did all that outside the religious systems of His day. He is our example and life, and He has not changed. He rebuked the traditions of religious men, calling them hypocrites and serpents for honoring God with their lips while their hearts were far from Him (Matthew 15:7–9).

People come to their meetings and have their minds eased a little from the preaching and worship, but such things are only superficial, a high that lasts until the meeting is over.

We must wait on the Master, pray to Him, and repent of our selfish behavior and self-seeking. We must know His will and walk and live according to His direction, not according to our own will. Help us, Lord, to replace our righteousness with Yours, our will with Yours.

The greedy assemblies of the sacrilegious magnifiers of men shall turn to ashes as their indulgence to incredulity becomes spiritual blindness and worldly wisdom.

Chapter Fifty-Four
Revival

I have heard of revivals in many places. Upon examination, I find only people who have been whipped up emotionally. They are like clouds without water.

Men continually try to change the course of history. Jesus never tried to do so—the world's times are in God's hands. Jesus said he couldn't do anything Himself, only what He saw the Father does (John 5:9).

Those whom God has chosen to be like Jesus will never be loved by most of the religious crowd. If they are loved, that means they've become like them. Which of the prophets were loved by such people while they were alive? Probably a few were.

God's gifts are to be desired, but why would anyone want them? Is the motivation to become notable and someone people look at with awe? I have seen such things, and my heart cries inwardly for it. Some people seek the gift of healing to become great among others, not because they want to cure the sick. Motivation is very important.

In the day when Jesus judges our motivation and not our deeds, He will say to many, "I never knew you" (Matthew 7:23).

Many are taught to study the letter of the Word without seeing the spirit of life and truth within the Word. They are purposely kept in spiritual infancy, dependent upon modern sons of Pharisees, taught only to listen without ever maturing spiritually. Where is the true church? Jesus said that wherever two or three are gathered in His name, He would be in the midst of them. That is very informal and very different from the teaching that says gaining wealth and numbers is godliness.

Ask the Lord whether you should submit to false ministries. How do we recognize them? They honor the rich, while God blesses the poor. They love great multitudes, while God looks toward the remnant.

God's Holy Spirit sanctifies us and sets us apart for Him. Sin is self-will, doing what we want, whether it's good or evil, and setting ourselves apart from God's will.

Has God ever revived a denomination? I can't think of one. God sends revival when people fast, pray, and wait on Him in true repentance. There are many schools of men, but there is only one school of life.

Do you want revival? If so, don't seek to be respectable. Instead, seek repentance and God's love.

Unity with Jesus in the Spirit is man's highest goal. Unity of believers in the Spirit is wonderful, but unity of vast numbers of people means little.

There is nothing so deceptive in man's heart than self-love. Man's pride draws Satan to him. Covetous, greedy men must someday leave everything behind.

The devil's cutting edge is man's anger and rage. The sword of the Spirit is God's Word and truth.

God saves some and teaches them afterward, while others He teaches first and saves afterward. He is magnificent.

Chapter Fifty-Five
Bible Schools

There isn't the vaguest mention of Bible schools in the New Testament. That is a man-made invention that cranks out, day after day, professional preachers speaking great words in man's tradition. The people are trained to keep vineyards the leaders haven't kept. They are taught to achieve, while God simply wants us to believe. Greedy preachers teach people to work and give, but they seek to build their own ministry. Under the veil of respectability, preachers learn about worldly things in their schools.

A preacher must reveal Jesus Christ as Lord alone and must not receive glory due to God.

Sunday schools aren't mentioned in the New Testament either. The twelve apostles were unlearned, ignorant men, but they were with Jesus (Acts 4:13). The only exception was Paul, and he considered his previous religious training to be rubbish (Phil. 3:4–9).

In God's school of life, He teaches humility before honor, the cross before the crown, death before life, and being broken before we can become whole.

The present-day hierarchy wants to maintain the old system and resists change. Jesus once spoke about new wine and old wineskins, while those in the hierarchy say the old wine (system) is better (Luke 5:36–39).

One of the first things Jesus did when He began His ministry was to drive the money changers from God's house. If He came back tomorrow, He'd probably drive out the greedy hirelings who preach for money, trying to increase their organizations while saying gain is godly!

Who is a false prophet? It's any preacher God hasn't called. Such men use psychology in place of God's anointing, using unknowing people as merchandise.

We must beware of scribes. Those were men of great reputation, noted for studying the letter of God's law. They hated Jesus, because He revealed their error, pride, and showiness. They loved their titles and having people admire them. Anyone who sets himself up as a judge over God's people is a scribe.

False prophets and scribes lack God's anointing and blessing. I doubt God will accept a ministry He hasn't called forth.

I must speak the truth as God shows me. I won't tease with words, nor do I seek followers. We should only follow Jesus.

Being with Jesus brings wisdom and knowledge.

I love you.

Chapter Fifty-Six
Antichrists

Antichrists aren't against Christ; they put themselves in place of Him. Any religious leader who is admired to the point of worship has just put himself in place of Christ. The more he teaches man's religious traditions, the more blindness to God's glory the preacher creates. All do such things in Jesus's name, stealing His glory and using His Word for their benefit.

If God is the potter and we the clay, why do we allow hirelings to mold us into their likeness? God is the potter, shaping us like Jesus. Our difficulty speaking—our deficiency in religious schooling—is what He looks for. He doesn't put new wine into old wineskins.

John, the Baptist, dwelt in the desert. He had no Bible school and was separated from organized religion.

Paul was sent into the desert of Arabia, while John was sent to Patmos, a desolate island. That was done so they could hear God's voice without babbling mouths bringing contradiction and confusion to them.

He still has a remnant in the desert, that men may hear Him more clearly and be purged of self. The Antichrists envy God's anointed and preach for profit, resisting those whom God sends.

"But why do you call me, 'Lord, Lord,' and do not do the things which I say?" (Luke 6:46).

Christianity is destroying itself through the traditions of men. John, the Baptist, said, "He must increase, but I must decrease" (John 3:30).

Today, professional entertainers and hireling leaders are increasing, while Christ is decreasing. After they speak from themselves, seeking their own glory, they use the name of Jesus to gain entry into men's souls.

Chapter Fifty-Seven
The Cross

What is the cross of Christ? It is God loving the world. At one time, many people thought the cross was a piece of wood, but soon the cross is inside their hearts, crucifying their natures from within.

Jesus's heart is very deep, and within it are His beloved ones, concealed from the world. Within His heart, the believer must embrace the Lord's suffering, loving His cross willingly. There are no nails holding him there.

When he is there, in the heart of God, he feels very solitary and abandoned. Then he cries out, "Why? Where are you?"

Quietly, unnoticed, he still embraces the cross; blowing any suffering for Him is great consolation.

The Lord is proving the believer's commitment apart from his brave words. The Lord has given him many blessings. When those aren't appreciated, the seeker looks for pleasure away from the cross.

Many are called, but few are chosen to go on that pilgrimage of devotion.

Blessed are the pure in heart, because they have willingly sacrificed their self-nature by embracing the cross and abandoning any desire for self-exaltation.

The calling is sacred and leads to purity of life and nourishment of the spirit. One surrenders all rights and fills his heart with compassion.

We must resolve to free our souls from worry long enough to meditate on the cross of Christ and devote ourselves to lovingly beholding His perfection. We must submit our will to the heart of the gospel, the cross of Jesus Christ, His death, resurrection, and ascension. That is God's power to man.

The one who sees the cross as only an outward expression of God's love to mankind two thousand years ago is a person who will be busy doing many works for God, trying to intellectually understand Him and His ways.

What of the one who embraces the cross within his own heart and sees it as an inward thing, not speaking to God of his own works or abilities? That one is blessed, because the cross made his heart pure. He knows the truth about himself, and he is freed from vain imaginings and the deep darkness of his will.

When one has embraced the Holy One willingly on the cross, he is truly with him and has entered God's heart. There, the soul forsakes the sinful water of the world and drinks deeply from the water of everlasting life.

The spirit of harlotry has corrupted many, because as they have sown, so shall they reap. They are enslaved by idols of iniquity within their hearts. They heard the wail of the shepherds who fed them for slaughter and felt no guilt. "Blessed be the Lord, for I am rich," they said. In the end, they will realize their works were worthless.

One should sow righteousness, reap mercy, and grow like a rose. The harvest is near, the winepress is full, and the valley of decision is approaching. We should let quietness and confidence in the Lord be our strength. The remnant shall walk on the highway of holiness. Good seed shall prosper, the vine will give its fruit, and heaven will give its dew. Rain will come, giving showers of blessing.

Holiness belongs to the Lord. The wicked will be taken captive by their own lust.

Chapter Fifty-Eight
Two Kinds of Light

There are two kinds of light. The first is divine, leading us to truth, peace, and serenity. The second is false light. Jesus warned us to beware of the light within that was darkness (Matthew 6:23). Satan and his ministers can appear as angels of light, but their light is artificial (2 Corinthians 11:13–15). They appear as righteous ministers.

If one is assaulted by false light, he should turn within himself to the inner citadel of light. God is light, and in Him there is no darkness. All one needs is the faith that He dwells within. He must believe He is there, and outward attachments to worldly desires will vanish. Light and darkness cannot dwell together.

Jesus is the light, and light shown from within Him reveals His divinity. The darkness hates the light, because the light reveals the false light, which is darkness.

The false light is very deceptive and looks like the true light, but it is a counterfeit. The only way to recognize the false light is to understand that it presents a distorted view of Jesus.

Quietly, with loving devotion, one should embrace the true light of God, letting it purge oneself. With pure love, one should give himself to Him, trusting Him to do His transforming work within. We should remain open to His gifts and virtues.

And as He prayed, the appearance of His face was altered, and His robe became white and glistening (Luke 9:29).

Chapter Fifty-Nine
The Way of Sorrows

The Christian who wishes to be in the heart of God should be prepared to follow after Jesus in the way of tears. There's no outward beauty on that way. It is the way of sorrows and grief, the way of being despised and rejected by men and, at times, feeling forsaken by God.

The way of sorrows will lead the believer to green pastures and still waters and, eventually, to God's holy sanctuary.

The world is desolate, a vast wasteland away from God's holiness. As we journey through that wilderness, His shield of salvation illuminates the world's darkness. The burning wind of fire shall purge the wicked from the righteous.

While others are honored for being Christian, our honor is to be crucified with Jesus. While others seek knowledge, we appear ignorant. Others seek to be wealthy and known, but we seek only His will and to rejoice that He has chosen us.

Chapter Sixty
The Chamber of the Lord

Only spiritual virgins can enter the chamber of the Lord and then only by invitation. The virgin's eyes are only for Him, and she is sick at heart when she is away from Him. Her love awakens at his touch. She is in the secret places of the cliff of the rock of her salvation within His chamber.

Suddenly, she senses He has departed, and she searches for Him. She dares not stir or waken her Love until the Beloved One touches her again.

The day breaks. Shadows flee, and her heart is ravished. Then He is back. He smells like cinnamon and spice, and His lips drip with honey. He knocks at the door of her heart and says, "Open for Me, My love."

She opens, and He comes in. Finally, they are one. His hair is wavy and raven black. His eyes are like those of a dove, and He is lovely and perfect. His desire is for her alone.

When he speaks to her, tenderly and softly, His breath smells of apples, and His desire is only for her. She is His bride. From His chamber can be seen gardens and orchards filled with fruit trees. Pools water the groves.

He has whispered to me about you. He has compassion and love for you too. Come to Him. He has showers of blessings for you, because He takes pleasure in you and will beautify you with salvation. It's jubilee time.

If He invites you, will you also come into His chamber?

"For as a young man marries a virgin, so your sons marry you; And as the bridegroom rejoices over the bride, so shall your God rejoice over you" (Isaiah 62:5).

Chapter Sixty-One
Mortify Attachments

Never desire anything too greatly, because then the gift of God's grace and peace will be lost. Greedy, prideful people are never at peace. Desire only what God wants you to have. Many things lead to bondage. Don't love things and use people—love people and use things.

Embrace wisdom, and she will be good to you. God can teach eternal truths quickly better than years of study. He teaches without babbling words or ambitions of men, who always have contentions and confusion. To be taught of God, one must not seek Him for what one can get out of Him; one must love Him for who He is.

I know someone who, by loving Him, has come to know divine mysteries—not by study, but by love. God reveals wonders by signs and, to some, by an inner light. That person saw others become recognized while he went unnoticed. Others found success, while he found failure. Others spoke great words, but his were quiet and fell on deaf ears.

One day, he said, "Lord, I want to die."

"That also is what I want for you," the Lord replied. "Now we agree."

The man was despised, rejected, insulted, and abandoned by his so-called friends.

That is a bitter chalice to drink, but it must be drunk to the last drop. The glory of God awaits those by the way of the cross. They shouldn't fear it or run from it, because it will stop their rebellion against God's will. Mortify anything that makes one a slave to sin.

Chapter Sixty-Two
Spirituality

To be poor with Christ is greater than to be rich without Him. Possessing Him is like having heaven. Man's pride seeks to possess things for himself, and his flesh can't obey God or even be subdued by Him. The only way to overcome such pride is through the humility and humbleness of Jesus.

Pride in ourselves and selfish love keep us from submitting to God's will. Jesus submitted Himself to man, because that was his Father's will. For all His work, He received only ingratitude. For the miracles He performed, He received blasphemy. Finally, He was reproached for teaching.

Men labor for earthly things and recognition, but they give little thought to the loss of their souls. They find later there was no profit in what they did, while the things that were truly necessary were overlooked.

There is something far greater than possessing grace, and that is to desire it with humility and patience. In so doing, one might break himself of himself and reveal his weaknesses. The weakness might not be what he first imagined. It's the thought of being wise in his mind that doesn't allow him to be ruled by others.

True spirituality isn't revealed in one's social position or in one's knowledge of the scriptures; it shows in true humility and love that seeks only to please God and forsake all worldly learning about Him. Be still, and know He is God.

Chapter Sixty-Three
Silence and Solitude

The more I listen to men, the more I become like them. I have found that when I avoided the idle talk of men, I was able to commune with God in secret. During those times, not many words were said, and the truth was revealed from within. There was a moving forward toward Jesus, but it was done secretly and in silence. Afterward, it was easier to see the presumption and pride of the deceivers.

No one can remain there if he's conscious of himself. He must renounce his will and kill all passions, appearing as a fool for Christ.

It seems that before one can reach such a place, a mist of death covers him to remove flesh and offenses. A sense of victory over oneself appears, and there's the feeling of being a stranger in the world. All things seem to be coming to an end. Only the inward man understands that, because the outward man is drawn to the world and is entangled in himself.

The tree of knowledge of good and evil has deceived many. I have found that all men pretend to be good and appear that way, but in the end, they act for themselves. Jesus, as the tree of life, has no such deceits. He is pure, and his fruits are graceful. The deceitful tree, which is Satan, doesn't want to die but creates its own death anyway.

Those deceivers seek their own interests and use people for their benefit, but those of the true tree of life take no thought for themselves as they seek the profit of many. Deceivers receive honor and respect, while Christians honor God and give glory to Him.

Deceivers are afraid of being put to shame and are disturbed by losses. They are covetous and prideful of their positions and accomplishments. They seek praise and admiration, and everything they do is for their own gain.

Truly devout Christians gladly suffer reproach for Christ and aren't upset over losses. They are content to receive comfort from God and reflect His image daily. They see the virtue of patience, humility, obedience, and striving for closer union with God to be transformed by His love. By the gift of God's grace, they conquer themselves and their fear of suffering.

> And you have done worse than your fathers, for behold, each one walks according to the imagination of his own evil heart, so that no one listens to Me. (Jeremiah 16:12)

Chapter Sixty-Four
Divine Justice

If one would seek wisdom from God, he must first learn to fear God and His holy justice. Men have been misguided and blinded to God's divine justice.

All that is good on earth is a small reflection of God. Man was made for heaven, but sadly, many won't go, because they have sinned. Hell was made for the devil and the fallen angels. The choice is man's.

There are no words to describe hell. There are no friends in hell, no rest, no end to suffering, no comfort, and no end to torture. The fires of hell burn constantly, and there is no hope. Each sin has its unbearable suffering. Those who were greedy will always feel want. The prideful will be humbled, and there will be hard work for the slothful.

The greatest despair in hell is knowing God is lost forever. Hell is the home of torment, suffering, and despair. Souls are on fire there, crying out in horror.

Hell is a real place. Jesus referred to it often. He spoke more of hell than of heaven. It isn't pleasant to talk about hell, but it's necessary.

Have you been deceived by your desires, entangled by sin, surrounded by temptation, tormented by hidden snares, and discouraged by troubles? Are you tired of the misery of earthly life?

Look past the darkness. There is a bright morning star waiting for you. Put your trust in Jesus Christ as Lord. Only He can save you.

Chapter Sixty-Five
Pious, Mercenary Christians

True happiness isn't found in money, power, or fame. It isn't found in sex or in satisfying, lustful desires. Those things bring—in disguise—fear, worry, and stress.

One should set his desires on heavenly things. Many desire God's gifts, pleasure, and power. Few desire His cross. Many desire His peace, but few desire to suffer for Him.

When a man becomes a soldier and is interested in money, he becomes a mercenary. How many Christians follow Christ for what they hope to get from Him? They are selfish followers, and they are devoted to Him only for His gifts. They love Him for what they can get. They do good, but they hold self-interest in the background, coming to Him to avoid hell.

There is a remnant God has chosen to follow Him. They are devoted to pleasing Him always, having put aside worldly desires in order to be united with Him. They have drawn close to God's heart. They aren't self-made; they are God-made. They know all God's graces are gifts from Him to glorify Him.

May we become part of that truly devout remnant.

"Men of corrupt minds and destitute of the truth, who suppose that Godliness is a means of gain. From such withdraw yourself" (1 Timothy 6:5).

Chapter Sixty-Six
Divine Lodestone

To love is to possess life, because God is love and, in Him, there is no death. To love not is to possess death, because the light of God's love overcomes death.

Sometimes, as God wills, He quiets my soul into still, calm waters. He draws me into His secret chamber, and there, in silent adoration, I fall down before Him as a token of simple homage to commune with the Holy One. The calm is so sublime that I can only weep, overcome by His ministry of love and songs of deliverance.

Nothing cleans souls like communing with God. The most perfect love I ever experienced has been with Jesus. His divine lodestone is deposited in our spirit to draw us to His most precious love. Contemplate His humility. He loved his disciples and those who hated Him.

Giving costs. It cost God His only Son. Giving without cost means little. If one truly loves God, it'll cost him something—himself. He should open his heart to the divine nature of Jesus, and He will visit him, making His home within. He will never leave. Eventually, one's heart will be His dwelling place, a sacred shrine of His grace.

What displeases Jesus more than the sins of the flesh? It's secret pride in man's heart, which produces audacious, brazen rantings from harlequin-hireling Pharisees (Matthew 23).

What pleases Jesus? It's learned and willing obedience from the heart (Romans 6:17). Jesus always did the things that pleased the Father (John 8:29), and He is our life and model.

Chapter Sixty-Seven
The Fire of God's Love

O Lord of mercies, sweet and loving, accept as a small outward sign my devotion to You. My weaknesses are well-known to You. Comfort me, dear, patient Jesus, and surround me with Your boundless love. You alone are the king of true glory. You alone are the model of true holiness. You alone are the all-perfect God, the source of all good. Forgive me for my foolish pride and blind self-love. Protect me from self-seeking and the many forms of self-deception.

I place my heart at Your feet. Enlighten it to appreciate more of Your infinite consolations. I am poor in virtues and need your tender mercies and the fire of Your love. You alone are my food and drink. You alone are my love and joy. You alone are my life.

Unite me with yourself. Transform me into Your image and purify my heart with the fire of Your love. May your wisdom flood my soul as it descends upon me to replenish my heart by Your grace. You alone are the strength of my life. Although I was a little spark hidden in the ashes, the fire of Your love became monastic to me. You alone are the teacher of discipline, the one who gives birth to tears. You are a man of sorrows, the healer of afflictions, and the light of the world.

You are God, and I am devoted to You.

Chapter Sixty-Eight
The Voice of Melody

Man has two choices—either God is, or He isn't. If He isn't, then there is no good, no hope, no love, and no heaven. That leaves us like dogs in the streets.

If God is and one believes that through Christ Jesus, there is heavenly peace and light, then there is hope and life. One's life will be as a song to God, a voice of melody more delightful than the call of a nightingale. Our song will make beautiful melodies in heaven and echo throughout eternity. As we live in harmony with the divine Jesus Christ, He quietly begins to conform us to Him, guiding and sustaining us, taking possession of us, and becoming the guide of our soul.

He gives us all good things for our benefit. He gives himself to us totally that we may possess Him and reflect His glory.

Let your heart be filled with hope, because He holds the future in His hands. May He grant you a divine visitation. Don't listen to doubt. God loves you and wants to communicate with you in many ways. Seek Him. He waits for you. Noble love and serenity await you. Listen quietly to the voice of melody singing His sweetness and goodness. He is waiting for you.

Chapter Sixty-Nine
True and False Salvation

True salvation lies only in Christ Jesus. There is also false salvation from man, something many find it easy to believe in. Frail men, who deceive many, say, "Behold, here is the anointing!" They are tellers of tales, possessing crafty tongues and are devoid of truth. They are carried about by every wind of doctrine.

Crowds are moved by their oratory, but the kingdom of God isn't in words. It's in power (1 Corinthians 2:4). The crowds see such men as rich, powerful, great, and mighty, but such things aren't as they appear. They are temporal, uncertain in our changing world.

There are those who, if they are fed the needful things in life, wouldn't care to move on to heaven. If there is so little holiness here, why should people wish to stay? Many are afraid of dying, but it's hazardous for many others to live. They seem to be storing up wrath to come. They should live in such a way as to not fear death.

For those who have accepted Christ as Lord and Savior, they are pilgrims and strangers upon the earth. They don't belong—they're just passing through.

How would someone know if his pastor is a Pharisee in disguise? First, the pastor will separate himself from his flock and emphasize the traditions of his religious affiliation. Outwardly, he'll be careful with religious details, loving to display himself. He will be covetous of attention and appear righteous before men. He will be blind to deeper spiritual truths and will always seek self-justification by perverting scripture and hindering true believers. Such men love to be called by titles.

Chapter Seventy
The Blood of Jesus

The doctrine of life for a life is common throughout the Bible. It was God who first showed that teaching to man—Adam. Only by shedding blood could man cover his nakedness. The blood of animals was the first blood shed. Their skins covered Adam's and Eve's nakedness. Fig leaves weren't enough, just as fig-leaf Christianity—trying to cover one's sins by self-righteousness—is never enough.

A life for a life. The life of Jesus for our lives was the atonement. God said that the life of the flesh is in the blood (Leviticus 17:11), so whose blood did Jesus have? The Holy Spirit overshadowed Mary, and God's seed was deposited in her. In natural conception, the son has his father's blood.

The blood of Jesus was without sin. It was, and is, holy and precious. Jesus is God. He was a man as we are, but His blood was innocent. Ours is not.

Jesus's blood says, "Atonement. Sin is covered. Sin is taken away. Mercy, grace, and love."

Abel's blood cried out for vengeance (Genesis 4:10). Demons flee at the blood cry of Jesus. We too should plead the blood of Jesus. It is final, sufficient, conquering, innocent, precious, necessary, and cleansing. It gives eternal life, reconciliation, redemption, sanctification, justification, communion, and victory.

Whose blood did Jesus have? Was it the blood of … God?

Chapter Seventy-One
Lust

Lust is *L*ucifer's *u*surping *s*anctified *t*raining. It's evil desire that Satan puts in men's hearts, making it enticing, harmful, and always deceitful.

There is a point at which God will turn a person who lives and walks in lust over to it as punishment (Romans 1:24–32). Many false teachers indulge in it and are received by the multitudes, walking in accordance to their lust, scoffing at those who warn of the last days (2 Peter 3:3).

What should a Christian do? He must flee lust and not carry it out. Although he once lived in it, he must consider himself dead to it.

Men don't just lust after sex; they also lust after power, recognition, preeminence, reputation, money, and selfish ambitions. Such temptation can reveal to a man just what is in himself, driving him to the cross of Jesus Christ for forgiveness and mercy.

Lust is the counterfeit of God's love. Lust is an enemy that never rests. Only by God's grace can we conquer it. God's grace means we get what we don't deserve—heaven. God's mercy means we don't get what we do deserve—hell.

God is wonderful. He has given us gateways to the soul through our eyes, ears, and feelings. We can use those gateways for reading His Word, listening to His voice, or feeling His presence.

Jesus also warned us to beware of what we look at. If we look at things that are holy and good, our body will be filled with light. If we look at things that are bad and evil, our body will be filled with darkness (Matthew 6:22–23). He said his sheep hear His voice (John 10:16) and they follow Him. They will also hear and understand Him (Matthew 13:14–16), but the wicked won't see, hear, or understand.

Lust is attached to flesh, self, and the devil. Love is attached to God's spirit and all that is good and holy. God is love.

What if, after God saved us, we were never tempted by lust, we never sinned, and we never transgressed God's law? We would eventually become filled with pride and stop going to God. We might even think we could be as Him. The first lie the serpent told man was "You will be like God, knowing good and evil" (Genesis 3:5).

After God has done so much for us, we sin. That should drive us to Jesus's cross to ask forgiveness and admit He was right. Only God is good. We aren't God. If we are saved, God dwells within us, but that doesn't make us God. It just reveals how wonderful God is to us.

Regardless of what the false churches say they are, they are loveless, corrupt, compromising, lukewarm, and dead.

Chapter Seventy-Two
Heavenly Visitation

At times of pure prayer, I can almost hear choirs of angels putting phantoms of the enemy to flight. Where a man's treasure is, his heart will also be. Those things, however, are seen dimly, as through a glass.

Recently, I dreamed I was in heaven, beholding the glory of His kingdom. I saw, among other things, that the buildings had no glass where the windows were. There were no doors either, just openings.

I asked the Lord why that was so.

"There are no covered windows," He replied, "because the temperature is always perfect here and there is no night. There are no covered doors because there are no thieves."

I looked to the right and saw fields of grass, trees, a meadow, and a stream. It was perfect. Everything was in harmony and in its proper place.

I turned left and saw the Lord.

"Some don't walk before Me sincerely," He said. "They are merely curious about Me and filled with pride. I am in their mouth, not in their heart."

When I woke, the dream remained vividly in my mind. Writing it down for this book is the first time I have mentioned it, and I hope, in some small way, my readers will be drawn closer to Jesus by my dream and heed His Word.

"These people draw near to me with their mouth, and honor me with their lips, but their heart is far from me. And in vain they worship me, teaching as doctrines the commandments of men" (Matthew 15:8–9).

Jesus called them hypocrites, which means actors. They looked like they were drawing near God by their sermons, honoring Him in their speeches, but their hearts were far from Him. Consequently, their worship was empty and meaningless. Their teachings were merely the doctrines of men—about God. The traditions of religious men have always been a hindrance to the movements of God.

When will men learn that it isn't their own efforts that count but God's choice? When will men learn that they can only live for God when they die to themselves? When will men submit to being disciples of Christ, disciplining themselves in speech, prayer, and how they live? When will men learn to discipline themselves to simple obedience?

Due to man-made doctrines and false teachings, the palliation of sin abounds today. The arrogant are called the blessed, the wicked are envied, and the defiant ignore reproof and are justified by excusing their sins.

May the anointing oil sent by God illumine our hearts and bring harmony, symmetry and set in order that which fulfills itself into perfect righteousness while receiving the image of the invisible God, the King of glory.

Chapter Seventy-Three
Anointing

God is love, so we must love Him then men He created. God is also fire, so our hearts mustn't be cold; they must burn with the fire of God's love and light.

There is benefit in all things God created. To take that good and receive it through God's love will fill the soul with sublime pleasure and contentment. God, who created our hearts, can fill and satisfy them.

Before we can reflect Him, the purifying work in the furnace of God's fire must purge the dross of sin from us. The image of Jesus is then reflected in us so that God can see Jesus as if in a mirror when He looks at us. This reflection is done through love, offering to God the fruit of our lips as our hearts swell with thanksgiving.

Each time we go to God, we reflect more of Him. This is done quietly, and He takes pleasure in it.

Quite recently, I was told that my first writings revealed some of God's power and that my second writings were His anointing. In all honesty, I can't say my in any of that. All that is good is of Him, for Him, and through Him and His glory.

True spiritual depths can only be understood and received by a pure heart. Knowledge of the mind rejects the mysteries of God.

Chapter Seventy-Four
The Holy Spirit

The Holy Spirit is the Spirit of God. He contains all holiness, truth, grace, and the glory of God. He is called the Eternal Spirit and is joined with the Father and the Son. He is eternal, omnipotent, omniscient, and omnipresent.

The Holy Spirit comforts us, strives with us, speaks, teaches, and helps us in our weakness. He can be grieved and resisted.

He conceived Jesus, filled Him, and raised Him from the dead. All scripture was written by Him, and He indwells, sanctifies, and empowers the believer. He gives gifts, joy and bears fruits for Christians. He reveals the mysteries of God and makes holy the soul of man. It is He, not man or his organizations, that appoints ministers in the church.

He is God, the Holy Spirit. He won't glorify Himself, but I will give him glory. Thank you, Jesus.

How is the Holy Spirit grieved or quenched? It isn't how many people think.

If I asked the average born-again Christian "Is the Holy Spirit welcome in your fellowship?" the answer would most likely be yes.

We sing praises to the Holy Spirit and welcome Him, then when He wants to speak or do something, we ignore Him or quench Him by controlling the meeting.

The disciples in the early church always gave room for the Holy Spirit. They never controlled the meetings. The fellowships were open to the Holy Spirit's movements.

Suppose I invited you to my home and said you were welcome there. Suppose that after you came to my home, I ignored you. Would you feel grieved? If I did all the talking, would you feel quenched?

Today, if one goes to a church meeting, he will probably be handed a church bulletin. In it will be a list of the pastors—by rank—just like an American corporation. Then there will be notes about what happens during the meeting. True to form, such things happen week after week, year after year. Then we are told there is freedom of the Holy Spirit!

Oh, man, do you see the brightness of heaven or the darkness of the sky? Out of His mouth proceed living waters. His breath is moist with life. For some, the waters become hard as stone, turning into hail and ice from God's breath. Such frost of heaven we call the solemn assembly. As the days of autumn draw to a close and the spring rains quiet and become few, look up. The flames of God's lighting will make the dark clouds shine with His glory. Amen.

God is a god of order. If the hirelings would yield to the Holy Spirit and stop controlling the meeting, maybe—just maybe—the Holy Spirit would manifest. The greatest fear that those who control such meetings have is that God might do something and not use them. It is very predictable.

There is authority that God placed in the church, but those who have truly received His authority would never try to dominate or control the church. They would use their authority to open the fellowship to the Holy Spirit and guard against deceivers and self-promoters.

God uses His whole body, not just one or two. If anyone wants to know what order in a new-testament church should be like, he should read 1 Corinthians 14:26–40. That shows how God uses the many, not the few. That is the Lord's commandment (1 Corinthians 14:37).

If people were humble enough to submit to the gentle lead of the Holy Spirit, everything would be decent and in order. There would be no confusion. The problem lies in a few hirelings who feel threatened about their position and salary.

"If anyone does not recognize this, he is not recognized" (1 Corinthians 14:38).

All that he does will be in vain.

Hirelings always desire recognition for their position.

Weep for yourselves, you who have chosen men's traditions before Christ. The green wood, the life of the Holy Spirit, is dry, because you have calcified those sent to you. Come back to your first love.

Chapter Seventy-Five
Quiet Love

How should we seek the Lord? There are those who seek Him by continually receiving knowledge of scripture. They try to do some effort at revival or to destroy self or, worse, promote self.

The one who waits for the Lord to act learns first to quiet his mind then his desires in his effort to please his Lord. That quiet must be attained if one is to communicate with God, to hear His voice.

We must love him with our whole heart, not seek to exalt ourselves by being prideful at knowing God. True love isn't found in many words. It is in a pure heart for Jesus.

The woman who anointed his feet with her tears never said a word to him. Jesus said, "She loves me much." He saw her heart. Quiet love is deep and silent (Luke 7:36–50).

To communicate with God, one must love Him and wait for Him to reveal Himself. To know about God, one uses his intellect to read about Him. Do we love God for our own benefit or for who He is?

There are more Pharisees within Christianity today than there were around Caiaphas, the Jewish high priest during Jesus's time. We must remember that the earth is merely the earth. One day soon, it will burn from the flames of God's fire.

Chapter Seventy-Six
Interior Life

True devotion to Jesus Christ is manifested by obedience to Him. How can we say we are His followers and He is our Lord if we don't obey Him?

External devotion of Christ is manifested when we have fellowship with one another, because the external is a reflection of the internal. Interior life is divinely inspired and manifests through our patience, love, kindness, and lack of selfishness.

Interior life teaches us to get along without more of the world's riches. From it we learn freedom from wants and desires and not to consider ourselves too highly.

The interior life of Jesus teaches us not to excuse our trespasses, not to be critical of others while ignoring our own faults, and to remember how we hurt others while forgetting how they hurt us.

I have found it's better to have less than more, to do God's will instead of mine, and to be least, not most. Only God can quiet the storms within my heart and open the gates of prison to release me from my sins so that the dew of heaven may water my heart and calm my inner seas.

The shadow of our will and the darkness of our hearts are more harmful to us than many faults we think are greater. Only the light of God can illumine the shadows of darkness and give us a heart of flesh, pure and enlightened, rejoicing in Jesus and being one with God's mind.

Chapter Seventy-Seven
I Have Found

I have found that, on occasion, it's good to leave unsaid a word or to leave something undone if the Lord wills. Perfect love is Jesus. He is our example. We should examine His life and desire nothing but to please Him. Does anyone know when He will die? That may only happen when Jesus has perfected His love in us, and we should trust Him to complete everything. It is man's boastful nature that makes him want to complete everything, say everything, and do everything he starts.

As we grow, grace upon grace, we realize that so many of the things we thought important were, in the end, nothing but vanity and self-glory.

I have felt the cold, icy grip of secret gratification in others when I was humbled. I have felt the bitterness of selfish criticism and unfair judgment from prideful men when they wished to exalt themselves over me. I have felt the Judas spirit of betrayal from false brothers.

In all those, I also felt the kiss of God's love, being drawn by His grace, and in some small way, I have entered the glory of heaven, which is God's will. He sees men as pillars in the house of the Lord.

We should look through the flame and past the fire of His love into Jesus's face. There we see tender mercies and infinite love. He shed his heart's blood and gave His life for us. He is the Rock of Ages, the Lamb of God, and the Savior of the world. He is our heritage.

Chapter Seventy-Eight
Chariots of God

What are the chariots of God that carry us to heavenly heights and eternal life? We find them where we least expect them.

We find them in the depths of sadness as the Rock of Ages crushes our sinful natures to total death. We should set our ship on a straight course, and God's breath will guide us as the four winds of heaven direct our ship to safe harbor.

We live amid an unseen world, not realizing the spirit world around us. We tend to think that what we see is real, forgetting that all we see comes from the spirit of God.

We shouldn't weary our souls. Instead, we should let the quiet of our spirits and God's shining love conform us to the Savior's image as we reflect the light of His glory.

We should not glory in our own wisdom, power, or riches. We should only glory in the fact that God has chosen us, and we know He sends loving kindness, judgment, and righteousness to the earth.

The one who believes that Jesus Christ is Lord will have God dwelling within him. Such a treasure resides in earthen vessels, and we have cracks in our humanity. There is, however, a kind of brightness, a heavenly beauty. The divine nature reflects through our earthen vessels as His love is perfected in us.

Before we mount to heavenly places on the wings of eagles, we must wait upon the Lord to renew our strength and to allow His shining love to manifest as He wills.

Chapter Seventy-Nine
Selfishness and Pride

If a person lives to satisfy himself, he'll eventually become interested only in taking care of his own comfort without regard to others. He'll be concerned with his own interests and desires, seeking only pleasure.

He will generally put himself first, and such selfishness always leads to spiritual poverty and a spirit of mockery and worldliness.

If anyone suspects he is in bondage to such a thing, he can leave it behind by first seeking the good of others, then he must put Jesus first in all he does. Third, he can do those two in love, not because he must.

Selfishness is objectionable, unprofitable, offensive, and insufficient to the believer. The root of selfishness is pride, and pride manifests in a conceited sense of one's superiority. Such pride comes from Satan, who sends self-righteousness to ambitious people. It's a sign of the last days to keep people from going to God.

One thing prideful people always do is exaggerate their own importance and behave offensively. More than likely, they call themselves to high office in the church and then preach without God's presence or authority.

They also appear as holy and righteous, always doing something for God outwardly. They have a false ministry and will be denounced someday as sons of the Pharisees. Anyone not called by God is a false prophet.

> Therefore, thus says the Lord: "If you return, then I will bring you back; you shall stand before Me; if you take out the precious from the vile, you shall be my mouth. Let them return to you,

but you must not return to them. And I will make you to this people a fortified bronze wall; and they will fight against you, but they shall not prevail against you; for I am with you to save you and deliver you," says the Lord. "I will deliver you from the hand of the wicked, and I will redeem you from the grip of the terrible." (Jeremiah 15:19–21)

Chapter Eighty
Cross, Crown, and Crucifixion

The cornerstone of Christian faith hangs upon the cross of Christ. On it we received our reconciliation to God. The penalty for man's rebellion was paid in full to all who believe.

Jesus's execution on the cross was predicted by God's prophets and demanded by rebellious men. God, in human appearance, hung on the cross for man, whom he loved, yet was rejected by him.

I have heard Christians desiring different crowns they expect when they get to heaven, but I've never heard anyone ask for a crown of thorns like the one Christ wore. There can't be crowns without the cross.

We desire the crown as an emblem of glory, but we run from the crown of thorns that would mortify our self-centeredness and covetousness.

The new covenant was ratified by the Jesus Christ's blood, which He shed on the cross and offered to the Father. That offering was, for all time, for perpetual purity to the believer.

"Cover us, O Lord, with the covenant of salt so that we may not lose our saltiness" (Mark 9:49–50).

Chapter Eighty-One
Celestial Soda Pop

> For when they speak great swelling words of emptiness.
>
> —2 Peter 2:18

There are those who preach sweet little sermons who never offend anyone for fear the people might not come back. They give no real nourishment to the body of Christ. Those are false teachers, devoid of pure doctrine, who pervert scripture and preach celestial soda pop.

They look good outwardly, pretending to be innocent, harmless, sincere, and of course, led by God. They are always money lovers, bound by tradition and deceit.

The preachers of celestial soda pop have many flavors and always charge for their services, proclaiming their own importance. They praise one another and are always self-seekers.

One wonders where God's prophets are who would expose such hypocrisy. God's prophets don't fear false teaching; they expose it, as divine providence leads them to do. In so doing, they make sweet melodies and eternal harmony, echoing faultless music to God.

Let your heart be perpetually fixed on Him, and you'll look at things His way. His will, will then be done. He is our example, not man's rules and regulations. He seeks no one's head on a platter, just his heart. He will open, enlighten, and make our hearts pure.

Chapter Eighty-Two
Beginnings

What I am about to describe is something I have never told anyone before. It's sad, but through it, God was with me. He showed me what it was like to be scorned and laughed at and how to trust Him while going through it. He wanted me to be more like Him, not like man. I never had an earthly father.

When I was five years old, my father left my mother to live a life of the flesh without responsibilities. I remember that he was away for a few weeks then came back for his clothes.

I looked up at him while he shaved, hoping he would pick me up and hold me. I missed him terribly. "Daddy, where are you going?" I asked.

"Crazy," he replied. "Want to come?"

I started crying. I asked a few more times, but he always gave the same answer. He left for the last time without looking back, leaving me still crying for him.

My mother was the most tender, meekest person I knew. Her life was very hard. Father taught her to drink, and after he left, she couldn't cope with life. I saw her over the years waiting for him to return. When he didn't, she started drinking secretly. My heart was saddened to see her hurt.

I prayed throughout my childhood. "Dear God, please bring my father back to my mother."

My father never supported my mother or myself, and consequently, she took hard, menial jobs. Everyone looked down on us. Even as a young boy, I knew I had the best, most loving mother in the world. God used her to teach me about gentleness and meekness, learning to love those who laughed at the weak.

Even some of our relatives laughed at us. Sometimes, I took care of my mother when life got too hard for her. She was too gentle for the world. Through it all, she never turned mean or vindictive. She never remarried, and she loved the Lord the rest of her life.

When I was seven, I wanted to join the Cub Scouts. I saw other boys wearing those blue uniforms and wanted one. I waited outside the church basement when they met, hoping I might be invited in. I didn't think I was good enough—my clothes were like rags, and all the other children had well-to-do parents who lived together. I didn't know anyone else without a father.

No one ever invited me in. One Tuesday night, I went in. It looked good in there. The lights were bright, and there men were helping the boys. I wanted a man to help and welcome me too.

Finally, a man saw me and came toward me with a smile. I was excited, but my hands were dirty, so I shoved them into my pockets.

He put his hand on my shoulder. "You're not our kind. Please leave."

I went outside to the next building and crawled inside the bushes, wishing I could die. I heard people laughing inside, so I ran home.

I saw my mother looking out the window. She'd been crying too. That was a common sight.

I was also sent home from school because my clothes weren't up to standard.

My one bright spot came in the fifth grade. For the first time, a teacher took an interest in me. She helped me a great deal. I decided that if she thought I was worth something, perhaps I could finally join the Boy Scouts.

I decided to attend the next Scout meeting. They met in the high school gym. I was eleven years old then. I washed my hands and face, combed my hair, and put on my best clothes.

When I walked in, I saw other boys I knew from school and hoped I'd be accepted. The boys were in groups of four making model airplanes. I went to one group, but no one spoke. I went to the next, but when I neared, they broke into laughter.

"His father's gone," one said.

Another said something too painful for me to repeat. I left.

I have experienced such pain from other people who didn't realize the hurt they inflicted. In some small way, my mother taught me to love those who would hurt me. She loved Jesus a lot. In other writings, I have revealed what happened when she died. I praise God she no longer suffers.

When I was nine, I had a severe toothache and had to see a dentist. My teeth were crooked and decayed. I sat in the dentist's chair and cried. They thought I was crying out of fear, but they were wrong. I was ashamed to open my mouth and show them my teeth.

All during my childhood, I never thought I was of any good. On March 30, 1978, I met God, my true Father. He has never abandoned me. He never ridicules me or laughs at me. My mother is with Him, and she no longer cries.

Because of the blood of Jesus Christ, I'm worth something, and I finally have my uniform. It's not blue like the Cub Scouts; it's white, washed in His blood.

As for my earthly father, I forgave him a long time ago. Everything has worked out the way my heavenly Father wanted, and I praise Him for being what He is—my Father. I have my Father now, and all I wish is to please Him.

"Where are you going, Daddy?"

"Nowhere, my son. I'm with you forever."

"Thank you, Daddy."

Chapter Eighty-Three
Content in Every State

How does someone know when he has victory over himself because of Christ dwelling in fullness within?

It's when he refrains from having his own way and submits to others' will and when he puts his ego to death and promotes others. If he has been greedy, he gives to the poor, and if men look up to him, he is quiet when they misunderstand.

What does it mean to learn obedience by the things we suffer? What does it mean to give Jesus thanks in all things?

One has learned his lesson well if he thanks Jesus for loneliness and suffering. It becomes a joy to know that God appoints those things to teach the believer self-renunciation and how to be content in any state.

What does it mean when we pray "Your will be done on earth as it is in heaven"?

No one knows what is best for himself.

"For we do not know what we should pray for as we ought" (Romans 8:26).

We should choose not what we will but what God wills. We must entrust ourselves to Him, knowing only He can bring us to perfection, reflecting His divine will and love.

The horror of evil has been conquered by our Savior. All glory be to Him forever. Jesus Christ is Lord. Amen.

Chapter Eighty-Four
Appearance

Some people appear to lack sense for Christ's sake, while others appear to have wisdom in Him. Some seem powerful for Christ, while others are feeble. They lack strength, skill, or aptitude for Him. Some seem eminent people, marked by distinction, while others appear to be clothed in shame and disgrace.

I have seen those who are poorly clothed, who hunger and thirst and are homeless. I have seen those who work with their hands and endure being defamed, making them seem like filth.

Those aren't mighty or noble people, but God has chosen the foolish things of the world to shame the wise, just as He has chosen the weak things of the world to shame the mighty.

God has chosen base things to bring to nothing the things that seem mighty so that no flesh will glory before Him.

If that is true, then no one should glory in men or be proud. What does anyone have that he didn't get from God?

"For the Lord does not see as man sees; for man looks at the outward appearance, but the Lord looks at the heart" (1 Samuel 16:7).

Chapter Eighty-Five
Rebellious House

It seems that there are those who are drunk with the wine of self-indulgence, while others stagger, intoxicated by pride. As a result, the eyes of the prophets are closed, and the seers cover their heads. The vision has been sealed. We lack true wisdom from the wise and understanding from the shrewd.

As much as pride and self-indulgence have intoxicated the church with the drunkenness of self, removing men's hearts from God, then deceit will prosper, and smooth speeches will be given. What is left is a false church and rebellious house.

God hasn't sent them, yet they run. He hasn't spoken to them, yet they claim to proclaim His Word, speaking deceit from their hearts. They love to wander without restraining their feet. They are worse than their fathers, men with stiffened necks who refuse to receive correction. They trust in lying words that profit no one. They are corrupters given to covetousness, not even knowing how to blush. There is no word of God in them, only wind.

They assemble in the houses of harlots, the false church, to commit adultery and to catch men with snares. They become rich and fat, appearing sleek. They speak empty words and bring forth iniquity. Occasionally, they point at the righteous and speak wickedness to the undiscerning. Their tongues mutter perversity, while their hands are defiled with blood from the iniquity of their covetousness.

Although they take delight in approaching God outwardly, inwardly, they are troubled seas that have no rest. They cast up mire and search for debate and strife.

Sons of the sorceress, offspring of the adulteress, children of the harlot, who do you scorn? The power of God's flame is near. I exhort you to repent, you who worship the work of your own hands. Scorners have delighted in scorning and have rejected God's counsel and reproof. God isn't feared in the assembly of saints who are being enslaved by the sons of Ichabod.

The rebellious house will do one of six things—obey or disobey God, accept or reject Him, scoff at Him or ignore Him. Disobedience will lead to judgment.

Come to the light. Come to the truth. Come to Jesus Christ, for He is Lord of all, and He will quiet you in His love. Soon, we'll serve Him with one accord, and affliction will be conquered.

To them that believe, let me exhort you to do three things—be just, love mercy, and walk humbly with God. I love you in Christ Jesus. Amen.

Chapter Eighty-Six
The Teachings of the Lord

The teachings of the Lord are like rain from heaven watering the dryness of my soul like dew. Sometimes, it feels like showers on the herbs and grasses of my soul, giving me direction and instruction, pointing to the Lord's greatness and perfection.

God is the Lord of truth and righteousness, and I know He desires to free His people, who have, at various times and places, corrupted themselves. He wishes to cover them with His wings as an eagle would do, to carry them upward to apples of gold in heavenly places.

Many are filled with sin, deceived into sacrificing to demons, not God. The Lord has hidden His face from perverse people who have no real power from Him.

Communion then Covenant with Wicked Blood

My prayer is that they would repent and receive the Lord's teachings and understandings before He surrenders them to their enemies. Their enemies dwell in Sodom, producing vines that reach Gomorrah. The grapes are bitter with the poison of serpents and the venom of cobras, and anyone who drinks serpentine blood becomes a child of the devil.

People should fear the Lord, who kills and makes alive. He wounds and heals. No one can deliver them from His hand. He is the one true God who teaches His children understanding.

In His hand, He holds a glittering sword to render judgment and vengeance on His enemies. His arrows will be drunk with blood, and His sword shall devour flesh.

I pray my readers take heed to my words. These are for their good. People should set their hearts on them and not be afraid. The way to God is always open. Come to Jesus. He waits for you, loving you.

Communion then Covenant with the Wicked Flesh

Many shepherds draw near to God with their mouths, but they are far from Him in their hearts. They have destroyed His vineyard by laying secret stumbling blocks of their own delusion. Their conception is evil, birthing viper's eggs, which they give the unsuspecting to eat. They make covenants with evil, bringing death, not life. They enlarge their bed with deceptive perfume, enticing the unaware into hell. They have defiled the ministry with deception by eating wicked, serpentine flesh.

Delight yourself in the fear of the Lord and rejoice in His exaltation. The day of the Lord is near, and He will be exalted in that day.

I love you in Christ Jesus. To all who are saved, the blessing of the Lord be upon you. May you be blessed in the name of the Lord.

To those who seek the Lord and wish to repent, come to Jesus. He will never fail or forsake you. He loves you.

To those who reject, God still loves you, and He waits for you, but for how long? Receive him before it's too late. Amen.

Chapter Eighty-Seven
Boasting

There is something that Paul boasted of that has been generally overlooked. He said he conducted himself in the world in simplicity and godly sincerity, not with fleshly wisdom, but by God's grace (2 Corinthians 1:12). People should meditate upon that verse.

So often, the gospel today is preached by men's wisdom using the persuasive words of human wisdom, which is the thing Paul said not to do (1 Corinthians 2:1–5). Such preaching is worldly and natural, sometimes foolish, and it always leads to self-glory. The worst part of it is that it deludes many and can't save anyone.

It is possible to recognize those who preach from human wisdom—they always have a secret strategy for calling themselves to the ministry. Once there, they assume dictatorial rights. That can be seen in Satan's fall (Isaiah 14:12–14). They follow in their fathers' footsteps, being crafty and poisonous, trying to secure men's worship by stealth. They disguise themselves as ministers of righteousness and angels of light (2 Corinthians 11:13–15). They misuse scripture for their own benefit, their hearts lifted up in pride. They seek to make disciples after themselves, and when they have done so, they want to rule with absolute authority.

Do you know anyone like this? Dictator or disciple, the choice is yours. Choose life—choose Jesus.

Chapter Eighty-Eight
Meditation

We must decide between sanctimoniousness and sanctification. The first pretends to be holy, while the second grows in holiness.

Hypocrites hide behind sanctimoniousness, loving to serve God in front of people so they can be seen and noticed. Jesus referred to them in Matthew 6:5. Eventually, their interest in externals produces corruption and rottenness, moral decay and ruin. They pretend to be holy but are bound by the traditions of men.

Believers are elected to sanctification, producing holiness that leads to fruitfulness, mercy, and God's love. Believers must meditate on God, His Son, Jesus Christ, God's Holy Spirit, His Word, and the life, death, resurrection, and ascension of our Lord and Savior Jesus Christ. We should quietly contemplate the eternal spiritual truths God reveals to us, then we will enter understanding and see Jesus crowned with glory and honor.

We should meditate on the cup He drank for us, the cross He took for us, the crown He wore for us, and the rejection and separation from men He endured for us.

Paul said he would glory in the cross of Jesus (Galatians 6:14), because he bore in his body the marks of the Lord Jesus Christ (Galatians 6:17).

We should contemplate Jesus's life, ponder His magnificence, and examine ourselves in comparison. We must make Christ our example then our life. He is filled with purity, forgiveness, humility, gentleness, and love.

Although we live in the days of grace, the believer will find the Grace Day a day of wonderment, astonishment, and amazement.

Please receive the gift of God's love, which was crucified.

Chapter Eighty-Nine
An Open Letter—Pride

Hello, Jack,

This is Rene.

I thought I'd relate what the Lord has been showing me lately. It's wholly your decision whether you read this for the body of Christ, but I believe He wants it read.

It has to do with pride within the church and how grievous it is to the Father, who sent His Son as an example in meekness, gentleness, and brokenness. We are warned about grieving the Holy Spirit, but the domineering spirit of pride within many Christians blinds them to true spirituality. The following is what the Lord has shown me recently concerning how to recognize it. It is very crafty, cunning, and deceitful, especially to those whom it possesses.

The first attack is with a thought, because pride doesn't wish to be revealed: *Don't read this. It's caused division. Rene's going too far. Play it safe. Wait. Do nothing.*

It is pride.

Pride always manifests in a conceited sense of one's own superiority. Pride finds fertile ground in self-righteous people who are ambitious and who exaggerate their own importance. Pride will attach itself to the gifts of the Holy Spirit, stealing God's glory while saying, "Glory to God!"

The prideful never know they are prideful, but they think themselves superior to other Christians, never equal. Have you ever seen one Christian talk to another in a superior manner? What makes one think God guides him better than the other?

Pride causes a person to attain a position of authority. Once there, he dominates those under him, secretly thinking they are inferior. A prideful person can't be taught or disagreed with. They look for sins in others while excusing their own. They can't hear God correctly, which is why Jesus said, "He who has ears to hear."

What I'm saying doesn't cause division—it will bring unity. Pride causes all divisions and dissensions. Pride in man produces lying wonders and counterfeit miracles while disguising itself as holiness. The prideful person will look at everyone else as inferior. As long as his ego is being fed, he'll like those who do so and exclude those who disagree, calling them divisive.

What's the remedy for such bondage? First, we must put Jesus first in all we do, not ourselves. Second, we must seek the good in others, helping their ministry. Third, we must do those things in love, not grudgingly.

Pride will soon cause a battle between two factions of the Christian church. The first group has a spirit of intellect from the tree of knowledge of good and evil. The second has a spirit of haughty behavior from the same tree. Both groups are conceited and justify themselves, saying they are respectable, cautious, and discreet.

Both are right; both are wrong. Each sees the other's fault. While they battle, wolves will come to hamstring both then scatter the sheep.

My advice isn't to engage in a battle with your brothers. Concentrate on winning souls, not arguments. If you do, the Lord will sort things out soon. None of us has the complete truth in our prideful little minds.

May we be seekers of the Light, not of the limelight.

Take up your cross, deny yourself, and follow Him. Don't try to lead.

Yours in Him,
Rene Bates

Chapter Ninety
Contemporary Christianity

Contemporary Christianity is filled with false prophets in sheep's clothing. Outwardly, they look like Christians, but inwardly, they are ravenous wolves. We can recognize them by the fruits of their lives. A tree is known by its fruit (Matthew 7:15–20). Are they filled with love, self-control, kindness, or are they full of selfish ambition, jealousy, contention, and dissension? (Galatians 5:19–23). That is the first way to recognize them.

The second way is by the doctrine they teach. They preach in the name of the Lord, pretending to be true Christians, but they preach peace and safety, the big lie, and corruption. They are unwilling or unable to repent and are very much self-willed. They are presumptuous, constantly overstepping their bounds and taking liberties in their supposed authority, which is actually audacity. They have forsaken the straight and narrow way, corrupting many by speaking words of emptiness. Jesus said that in the last days, many false prophets would arise and deceive many.

They are grace perverters, truth opposers, and money lovers, bound by man's traditions, deceitful, and deprived of God's truth. Modern Christianity is filled with eminent apostles of Christ who are false teachers of Nicolaism. They are pathetic philosophers who show indifference to the deeper things of God while defending their Pharisaic doctrine.

There is so much corruption in the church, and the time is so late that there is only one thing to do—religious leaders should stop their programs and all other activities and pray to God for Him to intervene and send forth revival. We must beseech God, crying out to Him in fervent supplication, admitting to Him our need for repentance. That should be done until the Lord reveals Himself. The flesh must die and not try to take credit for what only God can do. Most importantly, men shouldn't try to control God's moves. They must get ready to bid farewell to the present corrupt system and welcome a new move to God. They must drink new wine—the Holy Spirit—from the tree of life and His fruits. Only the blood of Christ can quench man's thirst for holiness.

> Merciful Jesus, summon me to Your presence and consecrate me with the sweet savor of Your gracious words, kindling within my heart the fire of Your love and the mysteries of Your wise consolations. When on the cross, You cried, "I thirst" and received sour wine. I thirst now to be filled to completion with your sweet, precious blood. Thank you, my King and my God (John 6:53–56).

Chapter Ninety-One
The Time of Distress

God will remove pride and all forms of self-exaltation from the church. He will also remove those who wouldn't accept instruction, who wanted to teach instead of learn. He shall send the fire of His burning indignation to devour the roaring lions and wolves who have profaned His sanctuary—those who wouldn't accept instruction and corrupted many with man's traditions. The same fire that devours the prideful will purify the hearts of the humble and lowly, and they shall be one. I urge everyone to repent now or suffer the Lord's judgment. Those who were outcast by prideful oppressors shall be brought in, and God will restore their blessings.

Chapter Ninety-Two
Autumn Consolations

May we be imitators of Jesus Christ, who came to us not as a brilliant philosopher or as one who argues His points to the glee of crowds, but as one who comes in simplicity, revealing the way, the truth, and the life. A person who possesses simplicity is very threatening to those who are controlled by hypocrisy, because even as Eve was deceived by the serpent's subtlety (hypocrisy), so our minds can't be corrupted from the simplicity that is in Jesus. He said we must be converted and become like children if we are to enter into heaven (Matthew 18:3).

Is there an order for those entering heaven? The proud, the respectable, and the discreet will enter in, if at all, behind the harlots, thieves, and sinners. I exhort all to the virtue of simplistic innocence, mortifying our selfish inclinations inwardly while receiving the autumn consolations of His holy virtues and bountiful fruits as He rains violets upon the saints from His divine lips. His autumn consolations bring illumination to the monastery of the heart, bringing light from the darkness and life from death. To indulge the flesh is to deprive the soul.

Embrace the cross of Christ, with all its sacrifices, trials, and suffering, because those produce shining tears of diamond. As He opened not His mouth, let us immerse ourselves in the train of His robes of the crucified during our time of direct communication with God, in silence and solitude.

May we cease to be a rebellious people, with a propensity for the idolatrous worship of men, prone to the heathen environment of the modern world.

I know many who are pregnant with pride and who are always having labor pain, but they never give birth to holiness, only wind and straw. Pride made the evil one fall from heaven. He was envious and became a subtle serpent filled with sinful venom.

Remember, dearly beloved, it was one act of love that put away sin from mankind, and He desires to be loved in return for who He is, not for who we are. We mustn't suppose that godliness is a means for gain, as many who love luxury think. We must receive His autumn consolations and heavenly nourishment during our sojourning from His sacred feet to His holy hands and, finally, into the most holy of holies, His pure heart. Few words are spoken during that journey, but many tears are shed by Jesus within our hearts, giving us living water and cleansing us of self-love. Oh, how wonderful life is ... and death.

There are two kinds of Christian service. The first is busy serving Jesus; the second rests at His feet. The first will end, while the second continues for eternity. It will never be taken away and is the only good and necessary part.

Awaken, O simple heart. The chains of the flesh are passing away, crucified by the love of Jesus, and the majestic autumn rains are just beginning.

Chapter Ninety-Three
The Sensual Gospel

Much is being said recently about the anointing, but few know how to discern between a true one and a false one.

A true anointing will never put on a show to glorify man as the false one does. There is no entertainment in it. The dishonest anointing gathers glitzy, professional entertainers to condition the crowd and put them in the mood to receive something they think comes from God. Such singers and preachers perform for their own glory, not for God's.

The false anointing is very predictable, telling the crowds weeks or months in advance where God will pour out His Spirit. True anointing waits for God and rests at His feet for Him.

False anointing produces false wonders and miracles and is a sure sign of judgment to come.

True anointing always leads to sanctification through the purification the Holy Spirit performed within the believer's heart. False anointing produces antagonism against true Christians and the light of God's truth. True anointing rests at Jesus's feet and isn't distracted by human preparations serving Him, as false anointing does. Those who rest at the Master's feet, listening, always receive criticism from those who are puffed up serving the Lord. They'll never be accepted or encouraged by those who haven't chosen the correct part.

So it was then (Luke 10:38–42), and so it is now. The intentionally inaccurate anointing will secretly preach a sensual gospel—their words relate to the pleasing of the senses and that which is perceived by the senses. The mistaken anointing will preach a defective gospel, producing within the unaware regretful, spoiled, unfavorable, substandard Christian behavior. True anointing will give birth to the genuine gospel, demonstrating God's celestial glory in all its magnificence and praiseworthiness. The false anointing, embodying mistaken ideas, will, in time, give birth to lowliness of spirit, darkness, dejection, and despondency.

The flames of God's fire will possibly melt some of the glacial coldness of the artificial anointings and put light on the darkness of the sensual gospel, bringing forth the river of life and the light of the spiritual gospel. Amen.

To those who have an ear to hear and a heart to understand, let me leave you with this: What we begin to see now is the deathwatch of the gloomy, deceptive, organized religious system. It gave birth to nothing but a dearth of life, religious institutes (mistakenly called churches), and canons of human pride, turning many toward insincere piety.

May the Lord Jesus Christ forever be praised within your hearts as He delivers us from the people-pleasing business.

Chapter Ninety-Four
Canterbury

Six months ago, I received a telephone call from the senior pastor of one of the largest churches in Nevada asking if he could speak with me. I sensed from his tone that it was a serious matter and invited him to my home the following day.

That night, as I waited for the Lord, I felt I should listen carefully to what the pastor had to say. The Lord wanted to teach me something.

At 1:00 p.m., the doorbell rang. The pastor was there, looking as if he'd been up all night. I invited him in and asked if he'd like a cup of tea.

We went into the kitchen. As I poured hot water, he said, "Rene, I have been a senior pastor at Canterbury [not the fellowship's real name] for five years, and something happened recently to shake my faith in what we're doing in the church."

"Let's go into the living room to talk," I suggested.

After we sat down, he said, "Last Sunday evening, after the service, I was about to go home, and a middle-aged lady came to speak with me. She said she had something to show me in the trunk of her car.

"I thought I knew her well. She's a professional person who dresses very conservatively and has a reputation of being an on-fire Christian. She's been coming to Canterbury for three years, and we've been thinking of making her a deaconess or putting her in charge of the women's classes.

"She asked me to go to her car with her, but after years of being a pastor, I knew better than to go to a good-looking woman's car alone, so I looked for the secretary. Luckily, she was in her office. I asked her to accompany us. As the three of us approached the woman's car, she began to speak to us.

"'I'm not what you think.' She put her key into the trunk lock and opened the lid, then she took out a satanic bible and spoke to me. I felt a chill go through me at her words.

"'For three years, I've been coming to your church just to see if you or one of the other pastors would be able to see through me. Three years ago, I wanted to find out who had more power, and if you discovered I was a witch, I promised myself to convert and become a Christian. Everyone in the church talks about power, but do they have any? I was almost hoping someone, perhaps an elder or a deacon, would see through me, but no one did.

"'While all of you were raising your hands, praying in tongues to Jesus, I was standing in your midst, speaking in tongues to Satan, sending out spirits of lust and division, which everyone was open to receive. You were even going to make me a leader in the church, because I played your game.

"'I tithed, was careful not to openly cause division, and told the church's leadership nice things, saying how anointed they were. Although I wasn't comfortable in your church, you were comfortable with me. I'm leaving now, and I won't be back, but I just wanted you to know how disappointed and hurt I am that none of you could discern me spiritually.'

"Then she pointed to her trunk, which was filled with occult paraphernalia. She got into her car and drove off, leaving me and the church secretary speechless.

"Rene, what are we doing? Are we just giving speeches? I'm very disappointed with the associate pastors. Why didn't anyone know about her? Is this just a Christian business, not a church? I feel embarrassed talking about spiritual power now. To be honest, nothing seems to be happening. What do you think?"

Immediately, I heard a sentence in my mind. "Call the elders and the church to holiness," I told him.

He looked at the rug for a long time, and I waited, letting him think. After a while, his eyes filled with tears. "They don't want it," he said slowly. "And … and I don't think I want it either."

"At least the Lord will respect your honesty," I said slowly.

He left soon thereafter. I doubted I'd see him much in the future.

Are you in church or in a charnel? Within its borders, the church has many charlatans and fakers, those who make a tawdry display of knowledge and ability. They allure, bewitch, and finally, captivate others, using amulets of pride and egotism. The members are deceived into thinking they're in church, but in reality, they are in a charnel—a place in which dry bones are deposited.

There is a love so deep that, at first, it seems cold. The flames of God's fire are beginning to burn. Amen.

Chapter Ninety-Five
The Finale

I have found, if you would have life, you must first embrace death to all sinful allurements. God looks with pleasure at one who carries His cross with dignity and grace.

From time to time, as my Lord wills, I receive a tremendous yearning to be encompassed by His love. It is as though the fire of His love inflames my heart with passions of burning affections, drawing me to His divine love. At those times, I can only offer Him my willingness to die.

If you also receive the heavenly breath and permit the virtues of Jesus, which are sweeter than ripe grapes, to be poured into your heart, it will be honey to your mouth.

I feel I'm gradually being cloistered from the world. This solitary monasticism brings about a divine sweetness. With His strength, I am able to immolate sinful desires to persevere and grow as a lamb among wolves. Just as our Lord was surrounded by adversaries, He was still able to touch our hearts by divine love.

Unforgiveness is like a rusty sword, severing relationships first and blood poisoning our peace second. It's only when we pardon those who offend us that we allow God to break the chains of hatred and bitterness. This allows us to be a more heavenly hammer to the anvil of the flesh.

It is my finale to worldly wisdom, and God's desire for me, to possess the virtue of simplistic innocence that leads me to be more like Jesus. I feel like letting go of anything the flesh would offer.

Over twelve years ago, I stopped singing publicly. Now, I sing privately, alone, to my Lord, for His ears only. My desire was to offer

Him not only my weaknesses but also any virtues or gifts. Maybe one day, I'll offer Him my writing—for His eyes only—and then the mist of my life. It has been the fruit of His tears.

Fifty-five years ago, God gave me the name of Rene, which means "reborn" or "born again."

Farewell, my beloved
Rene of God

The End

About the Author

At a time when divisions among the churches are subject to attack, both from within and from without, the author has felt led to write doxologies, essays, and thoughts. These words are a call to action to *all* true believers in the Word of God and can only create encouragement in the body of Christ.

After sixteen years of praying, waiting, and listening, Mr. Bates has recently completed two manuscripts for books: *God's Glory and the Exhortation* and *The Flames of God's Fire*. These writings are a trumpet call to holiness in the personal lives of all Christian believers and may serve as the foundation upon which a spiritual balm may be established.

The author's presentation of these sometimes-heartfelt and sometimes-straightforward and controversial beliefs have one common theme running through them: they come straight from the author's heart.

Warning! The books have a highly provocative and penetrating approach and will help the reader to think, reflect, and maybe even weep. Mr. Bates has been ministering more to his Savior than to people, though he freely relates his emotions and his feelings to those close to him. He was raised in Maine. After US Army discharge in 1968, Rene moved with his wife, Ms. Pauline, to Nevada, where he worked as a professional model, entertainer, and hotel host. Mr. Bates lives alone, with his cat, Coco, in Nevada. His wife, after breast cancer, went to live in heaven six years ago.

CPSIA information can be obtained
at www.ICGtesting.com
Printed in the USA
FSHW011255250919
62377FS

9 781643 494432